Boys, Girls and Achievement

Girls are now outperforming boys at GCSE level, giving rise to a debate in the media on boys' underachievement. However, often such work has been a 'knee-jerk' response, led by media, not based on solid research. *Boys, Girls and Achievement – Addressing the Classroom Issues* fills that gap and:

- provides a critical overview of the current debate on boys' under-achievement;
- focuses on interviews with young people and classroom observations to examine how boys and girls see themselves as learners;
- shows the impact of gender constructions on pupils' learning and behaviour;
- analyses the strategies teachers can use to improve the educational achievements of both boys and girls.

Becky Francis provides teachers with a thorough analysis of the various ways in which secondary school pupils construct their gender identities in the classroom. The book also discusses methods by which teachers might challenge these gender constructions in the classroom and thereby address the 'gender gap' in achievement.

Becky Francis is Senior Research Fellow at the School of Post-Compulsory Education, University of Greenwich. Her research interests include gender identity construction in education, gender and achievement, feminist theory and policy developments in nurse education.

Boys, Girls and Achievement

Addressing the Classroom Issues

Becky Francis

London and New York

First published 2000
by RoutledgeFalmer
11 New Fetter Lane, London EC4P 4EE

Simultaneously published in the USA and Canada
by RoutledgeFalmer
29 West 35th Street, New York, NY 10001

RoutledgeFalmer is an imprint of the Taylor & Francis Group

© 2000 Becky Francis
Typeset in Times New Roman by
Prepress Projects, Perth, Scotland
Printed and bound in Great Britain by
TJ International Ltd, Padstow, Cornwall

British Library Cataloguing in Publication Data
A catalogue record for this book is available
from the British Library

Library of Congress Cataloging in Publication Data
Francis, Becky,
    Boys, girls and achievement : addressing the classroom issues /Becky Francis.
        p. cm.
    Includes bibliographical references and index.
    1. Sex differences in education.   2. Academic achievement.
    LC212.9 F73   2000
    306.43–dc21   00-024907
    CIP

ISBN 0–415–23162–0   ISBN 0–415–23163–9 (pbk.)

For Sam

Contents

List of tables   ix
Acknowledgements   x

Introduction   1

1   Gender and Achievement: A Summary of Debates   4

2   Theoretical Perspectives of Gender Identity   13

3   Gendered Classroom Culture   30

4   Young People's Constructions of Gender and Status   50

5   Young People's Talk about Gender and Studentship   66

6   Young People's Views of the Importance of Gender
    and Education for their Lives   80

7   Young People's Talk about Gender and Behaviour   94

8   Discussion: Gender, Achievement and Status   117

9   Teaching Strategies for the Future   132

    Appendix 1: Interview Schedule   153
    Appendix 2: Transcript Conventions   154
    Appendix 3: Attributes of an Ideal Pupil   155

Notes   156
References   158
Index   165

Tables

2.1 Ethnicity and gender in the total interview sample   24
2.2 Classroom observation   25

Acknowledgements

This book would not have been possible without the co-operation of the staff and pupils in the schools in which I conducted the research. (The names of the students and schools are pseudonyms.) My observation of classes and withdrawal of boys and girls for interview was obviously one more hassle in an already pressurized environment, so I am exceedingly grateful for the friendly tolerance and co-operation of respondents. Warm thanks to them all. Thanks also to the Economic and Social Research Council for their financial support for the project. Some of the data in Chapter 7 have also appeared in a paper published in the *British Journal of Sociology of Education*, and I am grateful for their permission to reproduce it here. Likewise, thanks to Falmer Press for allowing me to produce some of the workshop exercises from Salisbury and Jackson's *Challenging Macho Values*. Finally, I wish to thank my colleagues at the University of Greenwich and elsewhere, and friends, family and Danny for their on-going support.

Introduction

Since the mid-1990s an increasing preoccupation with the male role has been reflected in the media and academic press. Extensive social and economic changes and the impact of 'second-wave' feminism in the second half of the twentieth century have led to a change in gender roles in Western society, most easily evidenced in the ever-increasing numbers of women now engaging in paid work (even after marriage). Yet, despite these changes, gender continues to influence our behaviour, choices and life outcomes. The types of work performed by men and women often remain distinct. Women continue to earn less than men on average, are more likely to work part-time and are dramatically under-represented in the most powerful jobs. The continuing assumption that male values and lifestyles represent the norm is illustrated in examples such as the lack of childcare provision in the British workplace. Further, gender roles in the family apparently remain largely unchanged, since women continue to perform the lion's share of housework and childcare (often in addition to their paid work).

But despite this apparent continuity in some areas of gender relations, an anxiety about the male role is increasingly being expressed. In the mass media the talk has been of a 'crisis of masculinity', the theory being that the traditional 'male breadwinner' role has been eroded by restructuring in the workplace and the increasing numbers of women participating in paid work. Hence men are left apparently bemused as to their purpose. Some sections of the media have used this account to explain male crime and increasing suicide rates. This focus on masculinity has been reflected in the academic press, with increasing numbers of researchers exploring the issue of masculine identity in various environments. And, crucially, in Britain this concern about the 'crisis of masculinity' has coincided with the increased awareness that boys have shown a relative lack of improvement at GCSE level compared with girls. GCSEs are the exams that pupils in England and Wales take in their final year of compulsory schooling. The publication of 'league tables', introduced in the 1990s to show the GCSE results of each school, has meant that gendered patterns in achievement at this level have become more visible. Hence the concern with masculinity has found its particular expression in the field of education in a debate on 'boys' underachievement'.

Such debates raise many questions. For example, are boys really underachieving? Media reports sometimes suggest that boys constitute a 'problem' (e.g. 'The Problem With Boys', *Observer*, 1999). Is this the case? What has led to the improvement in girls' GCSE results? How can any 'underachievement' be combated? And teachers and educationalists may raise the further question – why does classroom interaction remain so gendered?

This book attempts to address these questions. It does so by drawing on findings from a research project investigating gender constructions in the secondary school classroom, and on feminist and educational theory. The book describes the findings of a study that aimed to examine the gender constructions of 14- to 16-year-old pupils, with particular reference to the changing gender pattern in GCSE exam performance. Hence the study sought to explore how symbolic gender cultures, constructed and taken up in the classroom by girls and boys to delineate their gender identities, affected the pupils' classroom interaction and their approaches to education. Further, it attempted to examine the effect of these gender constructions on pupils' post-16 educational and career choices.

Having evaluated the evidence provided by this and other research, suggestions are made for future approaches and classroom practice in relation to gender and achievement. Regarding girls' outperformance of boys, the teachers' immediate concerns have usually been for practical suggestions and strategies to combat the boys' comparative underachievement. However, it is very important to identify and understand the causes of under-achievement before suggesting solutions, and this is something that many works in the area have failed to do. There is much confusion and contradiction in the literature. For example, some argue that the 'crisis of masculinity' is lowering the confidence of boys so that they no longer have the motivation or confidence to achieve, whereas others maintain that it is boys' very complacency and over-self-confidence that is causing the problems. Some of these hypotheses are based on sketchy or non-existent research. Conversely, many more theoretical works fail to engage with the lived reality of the classroom. This book attempts to take a fresh approach, seeking to combine theory and practice.

An evaluation of the extent to which the concern over 'boys' underachievement' is justified can be found in the first chapter. This chapter provides an overview of the debate on gender and achievement, and provides information on the economic and policy developments which have formed the backdrop to changes in educational performance. Chapter 2 explains the theoretical and methodological approaches adopted in the study described in this book. It includes a discussion of the notion of gender identity, explaining the theoretical position adopted by the author.

Chapters 3–7 are based on data from the study. Chapters 3 and 4 discuss pupils' constructions of gender during interactions that I recorded during my observation of secondary school classrooms. Here the various ways in which pupils construct their gender identity, and their incentives for doing so, are explored. Some of the consequences of these constructions for classroom interaction and pupils' status are also discussed. Chapter 5 recounts some of the pupils' interview talk about gender and learning, showing how pupils' constructions have become broadly more egalitarian, and how constructions of gender and the 'good pupil' have changed dramatically. Chapter 6 explores the secondary school pupils' ideas concerning the importance and impact of gender in the wider society outside school, and pupils' aspirations concerning their post-16 education and future work. It is here that the question of an explanation for the improved achievement levels of girls is addressed. In Chapter 7 the suggestion that boys' 'macho' constructions of masculinity are hindering their learning is explored in relation to the pupils' interview responses.

Having discussed specific issues around gender constructions, power and achievement in relation to the research data, the implications of these findings are evaluated in Chapter 8. This chapter explores the various explanations for girls' outperformance of boys at GCSE level, evaluating the arguments against the findings from the study discussed in previous chapters. Drawing on the findings from the data chapters, conclusions are made on the causes of boys' relative underperformance. The implications of these findings concerning pupils' constructions of gender are discussed, concluding that these constructions must be challenged in order to increase equity in the classroom, free boys and girls from repressive aspects of their gender identities, and to improve the achievement of boys. Following from this conclusion, Chapter 9 explores the various teaching strategies that might be used to address gender constructions in the classroom. The chapter evaluates the likely effectiveness of current suggestions for classroom practice geared at improving boys' performance and also offers new strategies and suggestions.

1 Gender and Achievement

A Summary of Debates

Much has been written recently about gender and education in terms of achievement and change. If we are to believe the impression given by the media, any gender disadvantage previously experienced by girls has now been transferred to boys, reflecting a whole new set of relationships in the classroom. Hence, it is argued, the focus of concern regarding gender disadvantage should now centre on boys. Yet a number of feminists (e.g. Howe, 1997; Francis, 1998a; Paechter, 1998) have maintained that gender relations in the classroom are actually characterized more by continuity than by change. This book aims to explore the construction of gender in the secondary school classroom, with particular attention to the issues of power and achievement. It attempts to demonstrate some of the ways in which gender relationships and power inequalities are maintained, as well as exploring apparent changes in these patterns. Finally, it discusses the disadvantages in the perpetuation of opppositional constructions of gender *for both sexes*, and explores methods by which the normative production of gender difference might be further disrupted. In this chapter the controversial issue of gender and achievement is discussed, to contextualize the research in current policy debates regarding gender issues in education at secondary school level.

Gender and Achievement

Gender and Achievement in the 1970s and 1980s

When some of the first studies of gender issues in education were carried out by 'second-wave' feminists in the 1970s and early 1980s, they presented a grim picture of rampant gender inequality in the classroom. According to this work, girls were marginalized and belittled in the classroom, the victims of systematic discrimination from male classmates and teachers and the school system itself.[1] The accounts provided in these studies resonated with female readers, as they reflected many of our own educational experiences. It was argued convincingly that the catalogue of discrimination that girls and women experienced in the educational system explained the low achievement of girls at maths and science in compulsory education, and the relatively low numbers of women progressing to further and higher education (Stanworth, 1981; Spender, 1982).

Many of these studies were particularly concerned with the role education seemed to play in reducing girls' self-confidence and feelings of self-worth and consequently in lowering their ambitions concerning continuing education and future work (Clarricoates, 1980; Stanworth, 1981; Spender, 1982). There was also a focus on the ways in which girls were persuaded, subtly or openly, that traditionally masculine subjects such as the 'hard' sciences and maths were 'not for them'. Many girls avoided such subjects, and when they pursued them their 'O' level performance was significantly lower than that of boys (see Spender, 1982). This issue particularly concerned some feminist teachers and researchers, especially because qualifications in these subjects are often necessary for access to prestigious and highly remunerated careers. In being channelled into arts subjects at the expense of sciences, girls were also being diverted away from high-status areas of future work (Thomas, 1990). Hence, programmes such as the Girls Into Science and Technology (GIST) and Girls Into Mathematics (GAMMA) projects were initiated to encourage female interest in maths and the sciences. Valerie Walkerdine (1988; Walkerdine et al., 1989) pointed out early on that perceptions of girls as 'lacking' at maths were actually grounded in fashionable notions of the 'right way' to learn maths: girls' learning methods did not conform to these notions and were consequently constructed as pathological by teachers. Hence, able girls were not being entered for prestigious exams. She and others[2] also observed that boys were underachieving at language subjects, and that this issue was being ignored. The failure to address boys' poor performance at languages while debating girls' apparent inadequacy in the sciences meant that girls were being unduly problematized compared with boys (Walkerdine, 1988). However, the relative lack of attention to boys' underachievement in language subjects was explained by the low status of languages in the public perception and in the curriculum hierarchy (and this was, in turn, bound up with the association of languages with femininity; Walkerdine, 1988).

The Climate of Change

The early feminist studies of education did much to raise awareness among teachers concerning girls' underachievement at maths and science and their low aspirations regarding post-compulsory education. The consequences of the often low expectations of teachers concerning girls and their achievement was also stressed. In Britain, many feminist teachers worked hard during the 1980s to introduce classroom practice with which to counter these trends, as either individuals or groups or as part of specific initiatives such as GIST and GAMMA (see p. 5). In some cases, programmes geared to improving equality of opportunity were taken up and implemented by sympathetic local education authorities (Arnot et al., 1999). Arnot et al. (1999) note the achievements of teachers in raising awareness concerning the discrimination against girls in schools. However, they also point out that these actions and strategies were never cohesively co-ordinated, but tended to take different forms in different schools, and were practised in some localities and not in others.

In terms of educational policy in the 1980s, however, equality of opportunity was not a priority (Blyth, 1992). Indeed, the Conservative administrations led by Margaret Thatcher in the 1980s and by John Major in the early 1990s often made this lack of concern with equity issues explicit (see Arnot et al., 1999). Instead, the changes in British educational policy at the time reflected concerns with 'standards'. The Conservative government was concerned that standards in British state education were deteriorating. It was hostile to the teaching profession, which it saw as undermining educational standards through the propagation of 'woolly' liberal teaching practices based on apparently left-wing concerns about equity and empowerment in the classroom. The Conservative administrations saw the improvement of educational standards as vital if the British workforce was to remain competitive with other nations in the global economy (Arnot et al., 1999). (These concerns continue to be reflected in the current Labour government's policies on lifelong learning.) There was an increasing focus on traditional whole-class teaching methods and the importance of the '3 Rs' (Francis, 1998a). This stress on the importance of 'the basics' and the drive to standardize education led to the Education Reform Act in 1988. The act established a compulsory curriculum for schools and introduced standardized testing of pupils in English, maths and science at different stages of compulsory education.

This meant that girls and boys were compelled to take the same subjects at school for the first time. While many commentators were concerned that the teaching of equity issues was marginalized by the introduction of the National Curriculum (e.g. Blyth, 1992), the National Curriculum served to ensure that girls could no longer choose to avoid, or be steered away from, traditionally 'masculine' subjects such as maths and science. By the early 1990s it became evident that girls' GCSE results in these areas were improving, and by 1995 they matched boys' achievements in these subjects for the first time.

The economic backdrop to these changing patterns in gender and achievement has been argued by some to account for the apparent 'crisis of masculinity' that men are argued to be experiencing. Manufacturing industry and connected occupations have been in decline since the 1950s, whereas the service sector has been growing (MacInnes, 1998; Rees, 1999). This decline in manufacturing has been particularly acute since 1979. Figures reported by Arnot et al. (1999) demonstrate that these changes are not as recent as is sometimes supposed: service sector jobs accounted for nearly 70 per cent of total employment by 1989, showing that a very high proportion of the restructuring of the marketplace took place in the 1980s. However, traditionally, manufacturing and industrial jobs are seen as masculine and are done by men, whereas the skills often required in the service sector, such as empathy and communications skills, are seen as being more feminine. For this reason the changes in the labour market are seen as having disadvantaged men. Certainly, it is the case that Britain is one of the few places in Europe where male unemployment is higher than female unemployment (though some female unemployment goes unreported, and unemployment generally is currently dropping in the UK) (Rees, 1999).

The decline of the manufacturing industry has meant that there are fewer traditionally masculine unskilled jobs available to school leavers. Such jobs required few (if any) qualifications and were the natural destination for young men leaving school without qualifications (such as the group of 'lads' studied by Willis, 1977). The decreasing availability of such jobs has led some commentators to suggest that working-class schoolboys now have less incentive to work hard because of the shortage of manual jobs on leaving school, and that this may to some extent explain their comparative underachievement at school (Pickering, 1997; Arnot et al., 1999). This argument seems slightly curious, as one could equally suppose that the lack of manual jobs not requiring qualifications could provide such boys with a greater incentive to achieve in order to access jobs requiring qualifications.

Gender and Achievement: the Current Situation

Against this backdrop of changes in the marketplace, and partly because of the impact of unofficial feminist projects and official Government policy in schools, the situation regarding gender and achievement at GCSE level has altered dramatically since the 1980s. Girls have been performing increasingly well in terms of attainment at GCSE level, and their achievements at this level now equal or exceed those of boys in all subjects (MacInnes, 1998; Barker, 1997), excluding some minor yearly fluctuations. This development has received widespread media attention, often being linked to the debate about 'boys' underachievement', which is discussed below. Owing to the rather hysterical nature of the response to this development in certain sections of the media, it is important to separate the facts from fiction regarding gender and achievement. Gorard et al. (1999) show that a lack of statistical understanding on the part of many commentators has led to a misrepresentation of the figures and a tendency to portray the 'gender gap' in GCSE achievement as bigger than it really is. Further, some question the extent of girls' apparent previous underachievement. Epstein et al. (1998) point out that in the days of the tripartite system, lower marks were accepted for boys to pass the 11-plus exam than for girls, supposedly because girls mature earlier and perform better than boys. Moreover, as Arnot et al. (1999) remind us, more girls than boys were gaining five 'O' levels in the 1970s and early 1980s, so in this sense they have always outperformed boys. Yet because girls tended to choose, or were steered into, traditionally feminine, non-academic subjects, such as domestic science and needlework, their 'O' level success was not viewed as significant. Their under-representation and performance at the more 'important', masculine subjects such as maths and the sciences was deemed more salient. And indeed, in the 1970s and early 1980s, fewer girls than boys went on to pursue post-compulsory education.

However, in the 1980s girls' exam results in traditionally male areas began to improve, and this was accelerated with the introduction of the National Curriculum. Girls have caught up with boys in maths and science, and are continuing to outperform boys at languages. Moreover, slightly more women now enter further and higher education than do boys (Department of Education and Employment, 1998a), more women than men get 'good' (first or upper second-class) degrees than do men (Higher Education Statistical Agency, 1999), and more women are entering the workplace than ever before (Rees, 1999).

Yet some gendered patterns in education have not changed. One of these is subject choice at the post-compulsory level. The National Curriculum compels pupils to pursue the same core subjects in school, but once compulsory schooling is completed pupils appear largely to revert to traditional choices, with girls tending to choose arts/humanities subjects and boys opting for science/technology subjects. Indeed, Arnot et al. (1999) and Rees (1999) observe that fewer young women are now enrolling on 'hard' science and information technology (IT) 'A' level and degree courses than a decade ago, despite a global skill shortage in precisely these areas. The sciences have a higher status than the arts in Western society, and science qualifications are more likely to secure a job. Moreover, this job is likely to be better paid than a job resulting from an arts qualification (Rees, 1999). Where men and women opt for non-gender traditional subjects at degree level, men excel compared with their female fellows, whereas women tend to perform poorly compared with the majority male group (Thomas, 1990).

In higher education, men continue to gain more first-class degrees and post-graduate qualifications than do women (Francis, 1998b; Epstein et al., 1998). And importantly, although women are represented in 'middle management' in increasing numbers in the workplace, they remain dramatically under-represented in top jobs and in the most powerful positions in society (Rees, 1999; Halford et al., 1997). Hence it is important to point out that although media reports tend to present boys as being disadvantaged in terms of school achievement, there is no evidence to suggest that this has affected their future career prospects compared with women working in similar areas. Indeed, shifts in the status, practices and gender make-up of occupations are taking place that are deeply worrying from a feminist perspective. For example, professions such as law and medicine have been losing their traditional power and status just at the time when women have begun to enter them in large numbers (Crompton, 1997). The association between greater numbers of women and a loss of power is also reflected in less prestigious positions, as many women holding non-management positions in the service industry are working in part-time, low-paid, and insecure positions (Ainley, 1993). (A particularly vivid example is provided by Fernie and Metcalfe's (1996) account of the rapidly expanding phenomenon of call-centres: in call-centres low skills are required, and a largely female workforce is surveilled and regulated to incredible extremes by mainly male managers). Indeed, some writers refer to a 'feminization' of the workplace generally, using this term to imply the loss of power and security that brings the conditions of male workers down to the level traditionally experienced by women. I argue that, when used in this sense, the term 'feminization of the workplace' actually has deeply conservative implications. Not only is it misleading, as the change in working conditions has nothing to do with gender (real 'feminization' might rather have increased childcare facilities in the workplace, for example, where despite the increase in women working there has been little attempt to accommodate their needs in the workplace), but, more worryingly, the term seems to echo the discourse of 'blaming women' (Epstein et al., 1998), as though working conditions for men have deteriorated because of the increased numbers of working women.

The recent media focus on girls' GCSE success compared with that of boys may in part be explained by the recently implemented policy of league table publication in Britain, whereby the GCSE results from each school are published. The availability, indeed prominence, of figures on GCSE achievement has highlighted the achievements of girls (albeit these may be exaggerated by misuse of the figures; see Gorard et al., 1999). Whatever the reason, the clarion discussion in the media and in the academic press of girls' outperformance of boys at GCSE level has constructed a discourse of 'boys' underachievement' (Raphael Reed, 1998). This discourse is by no means limited to the UK: it is prominent in many English-speaking countries (such as the United States, Canada, Australia and New Zealand), as well as other Organization for Economic Growth and Development nations (Yates, 1997; Epstein et al., 1998).

Evidence suggests that girls' improved achievement at GCSE level is the result of the removal of previous barriers to girls' attainment and changed expectations on the part of girls (Epstein et al., 1998). However, girls' improvements are often presented in the media as having been at the expense of boys. As Arnot et al. (1999) observe, the improved achievement of girls has been problematized, leading to the denigration, rather than praise, of teachers' success with girls. There is a tendency to imply that because girls were underachieving at maths and science in the 1970s and early 1980s teachers and educationalists have focused on improving girls' achievement, with the result that boys' needs have been ignored. Yet in fact, boys' GCSE results have also been improving year on year, although not as dramatically as those of girls. Epstein et al. (1998) have identified three separate discourses used in the popular and academic press to explain boys' educational 'failure': 'poor boys', 'failing schools' and 'boys will be boys' (they do not discuss pejorative narratives in reference to boys such as those noted by Griffin, 1998, and Francis, 1999a). The 'poor boys' discourse presents boys as disempowered victims, and this discourse blames females (girls, mothers, female teachers and/or feminists) for boys' apparent underperformance. Cohen (1998) ably discusses how low educational achievement among boys has historically tended to be seen as the result of external faults, such as the teacher, school, or method of learning or assessment, whereas low educational achievement among girls is perceived as the result of internal inadequacies. Certainly, there have been noticeably few attempts to explain boys' relative underachievement as being the result of inherent inadequacies, which was a reason previously used to explain girls' underachievement at maths and sciences in the past (e.g. their apparently lower spatial ability).

Hence many government and academic initiatives to improve boys' educational achievement are built on the supposition that boys' comparative underachievement is a result of a failure to make education sufficiently appealing to boys (see, for example, Clark, 1998; Department of Education and Employment, 1998b; Qualification and Curriculum Authority, 1998). Some commentators have also been quick to suggest that the increased assessment of coursework introduced with GCSEs has aided girls' success. Assessment of the previous 'O' level exam (which GCSEs replaced) was based almost entirely on examinations, which boys are seen to be more comfortable with. However, as MacDonald et al. (1999) and Arnot et al. (1999) point out, even with the reduction in coursework for GCSEs in the mid-1990s, girls are continuing to improve their performance: there has been no corresponding decline in girls' performance. Moreover, a large body of feminist research suggests that the school curriculum has always reflected and favoured the interests of boys at the expense of girls, and that a far greater proportion of teacher time and attention is spent on boys than on girls (Spender, 1982; Stanworth, 1991; Howe, 1997). As has been shown, this evidence was used by feminist researchers in the early 1980s to explain the underachievement of *girls* compared to the achievements of boys. Yet almost two decades on, research shows that girls' educational achievement has improved *despite* the continuing male dominance of the classroom, curriculum content (for example history's focus on the lives of men) and greater demands on teacher time (Skelton, 1997; Paechter, 1998).

A number of researchers have suggested that the discourse of boys' underachievement and concern with negligible gender differences in achievement actually hide far more substantial differences in educational achievement according to race and (particularly) social class (Griffin, 1998; Regan, 1998; Epstein et al., 1998). Certainly it seems to be the case that social class remains the most likely factor to affect one's educational achievement, and that this point has been persistently ignored by the media and policy-makers in recent years. Ethnicity also continues to have an impact, with the achievement of young people from different ethnic groups varying quite dramatically. Some researchers have suggested that pejorative narratives explaining boys' underachievement in terms of 'problem boys' are actually veiled attacks on working-class boys, because this is where such male educational 'failure' is located (Griffin, 1998). Others suggest that it is only since the achievements of middle- and upper-class girls outstripped those of middle- and upper-class boys at GCSE level that the discourse about boys' underachievement has become prominent, and that initiatives have been taken to combat the 'problem' (Yates, 1997; Power et al., 1998).[3] However, Arnot et al. (1999) observe that of all the inequalities addressed by educational policy since the Second World War, gender has shown the most dramatic shift in terms of educational equity. The issue has certainly become a preoccupation for educationalists. Under the front page headline 'Failing Boys "Public Burden Number One" ', Chris Woodhead (Chief Inspector of Schools), maintained in the *Times Educational Supplement* that boys' underachievement is one of the most disturbing problems currently facing the education system (*Times Educational Supplement*, 1998).

This chapter has attempted to summarize the arguments concerning gender and achievement at GCSE level, and to clarify the actual picture. The changed pattern in gender and achievement since the 1980s has been described. It has been shown that an account that presents girls as currently achieving and boys as underachieving is oversimplistic: not all girls are achieving, and many boys continue to excel at GCSE level. Factors such as social class and ethnicity also affect achievement. Moreover, stereotypically gendered patterns continue to exist in subject choice at the post-compulsory level, which influence young people's future experiences in the adult workplace. The results of male and female pupils continue to improve at GCSE level. Yet in general terms, it is certainly the case that girls' improvements have outstripped those of boys. The study reported in later chapters of this book attempts to tease out some of the explanations for this change in relation to pupils' constructions of gender identity in the secondary school.

2 Theoretical Perspectives of Gender Identity

This chapter sets out the theoretical perspective behind the study and data analysis, and describes the methodology used for the fieldwork. Some of the theoretical debate is quite complex (for instance, concerning notions of gender identity and discourse analysis) and might appear to some to be surplus to requirements in a book with a practical orientation. Yet I feel that the inclusion of such debate is necessary in order to explain the perspective I have adopted, and to apply this to consideration of the data on gender identity in coming chapters.

The methodology section is aimed at being informative, both in terms of providing an account of practical issues, such as the sample size and fieldwork methods, and in terms of the problems I faced and issues raised during the fieldwork. The inclusion of a (relatively) detailed account of my methods allows readers to reach their own conclusions concerning the apparent validity of these methods and their relation to the study findings.

Gender Identity

In the mid- to late 1980s, some feminist educational researchers became concerned that previous studies positioned girls as apparently passive in the classroom, providing a false picture of girls as submissively socialized into feminine behaviour.[1] Researchers such as Anyon (1983), Riddell (1989) and Lees (1993) showed how girls actively resisted the classroom regime, often using particular constructions of femininity in order to do so. They showed that girls' portrayals of femininity were not necessarily consistent and often contained contradiction.

Such findings, coupled with a dissatisfaction with the limitations of sex role theories and the influence of post-modernism and post-structuralism in the social sciences, led to a new interest in gender identity during the late 1980s and 1990s. In particular, researchers were interested in the ways in which gender is collectively constructed, and the various forms that such constructions take. Boys' 'underachievement', and a discourse of a 'crisis of masculinity' resulting from the changing role of women in society and the reduction in traditionally male manual work, has led to a new but burgeoning interest in masculine identity. This body of research work includes many studies of masculinity in the classroom. Much of this work on masculinity and education has drawn on feminist work and adopts a feminist or pro-feminist perspective. Yet as Skelton (1998) observes, a significant portion of this work on masculinity makes little acknowledgement of previous feminist work on gender and sometimes perpetuates the 'poor boys' discourse described by Epstein et al. (1998). Moreover, a preoccupation with the issue of identity has sometimes been at the expense of any analysis of *power* in gender relations (Skelton, 1998).

However, the focus on identity has been useful in drawing attention to the fact that presentation of gender is not monolithic. The individuals constituting the groups referred to as 'the girls' and 'the boys' have different ethnic, class and sexual identities, as well as different characteristics traditionally attributed to 'personality', such as charisma, confidence etc. This recognition of diversity has led many researchers of gender identity to refer to 'masculinities' and 'femininities' in plural, rather than to 'masculinity' and 'femininity' in order to reflect the different ways in which masculinity and femininity are constructed by different individuals. However, such concepts inevitably evoke typologies, directly or by suggestion. In educational research, for example, Mac an Ghaill (1994) and Sewell (1998) list various types of masculinity that they saw boys take up in the secondary school. Mac an Ghaill lists four types of masculinity ('macho lads, 'academic achievers', 'new enterprisers' and 'real Englishmen'), and Sewell counts four types of masculinity constructed by Afro-Caribbean boys ('conformists', 'innovators', 'retreatists' and 'rebels'). Reay (1999) describes different groups of girls in her investigation of femininities in the primary school as 'spice girls', 'nice girls' and 'tomboys'.

I do not draw on this notion of masculinities or femininities for two reasons. First, to suggest that there are different categories of masculinity or femininity, often with a 'hegemonic masculinity/femininity', at the top of a hierarchy and other forms of masculinity or femininity below (e.g. Connell, 1995) suggests something more fixed than is the case. As Kerfoot and Whitehead (1998) point out, the notion seems to reify gender as something fixed that can be dissected and categorized. Although categories such as 'macho lads' and 'academic achievers' (Mac An Ghaill, 1994) effectively illustrate the manner in which boys construct masculinity in very different ways, they also create new boxes, which individual pupils do not conform to all of the time.

Second, such categorizations raise problems with the very concepts of masculinity and femininity. As MacInnes (1998) has noted, these are purely notional concepts. He argues that there appears to be a conflation of gender and sex underlying writing on masculinities and femininities. 'Sex' refers to the biological differences between men and women (which, as Davies (1989) and Butler (1990) have pointed out, are actually often less fixed and clear-cut than we tend to imagine). 'Gender' (masculinity and femininity) refers to the social construction of differences in behaviour according to sex. MacInnes argues that none of the writers that use typologies of masculinity actually explains what these various 'masculinities' hold in common. MacInnes surmises that, "it is difficult to avoid the conclusion that all they have in common is possession of a penis" (p. 63). This ties the expression of masculinity (or femininity) back to essential sex differences; something that most social constructionists would wish to avoid. I argue instead that there is one (notional) masculinity and one (notional) femininity, constructed as oppositional to one another, and consequently shifting, but flexible, and incorporating contradiction (Francis, 1998a). Masculinity and femininity may be constructed slightly differently by different individuals, but in Western society are constructed as bearing some or all of the dichotomous attributes:

Masculine	*Feminine*
Rationality	Emotion
Strength	Frailty
Aggression	Care
Competition	Co-operation
Mind	Body
Science	Nature/arts
Activity	Passivity
Independence	Dependence

Davies (1989; 1993) has shown how gender is seen and felt to be integral to a successful social identity. Consequently, she argues, the taking up of a gendered identity becomes extremely important for young children, who go to extraordinary lengths to maintain gender boundaries. The same core values lie behind all constructions of masculinity or femininity, otherwise there would *be* no recognized masculinity or femininity (the boundaries of which are anyway blurred and contain contradiction). Of course no-one bears all those traits listed above as being masculine or feminine to the exclusion of others, and also different individuals may have different resources at their disposal in terms of 'doing' masculinity or femininity. Gender identity can be constructed differently in different cultures and social classes. Further, physical or other differences may make it difficult for individuals (for example physically weak men, or women who do not want children) to conform to particular aspects of the gender dichotomy. They may therefore use different strategies (consciously or subconsciously) in their ways of 'doing' gender. For example, if the weak man was bright, he might express competition and aggression intellectually rather than physically. This seems to have been the strategy of Mac an Ghaill's 'Real Englishmen', who scorned the physicality of the 'macho lads' but delighted in intellectually challenging and 'besting' their teachers. Indeed, although the different groups of boys in Mac an Ghaill's (1994) study clearly had different strategies and resources for constructing their masculinity, competition, derision and aggression appeared to figure broadly in the majority of constructions. Likewise, the traits that Arnot et al. (1999) list as associated with apparently separate 'gentry', 'middle-class academic' and 'new boys' masculinities actually overlap extensively. The slight differences (for example 'strength' might be expressed as control and emotional restraint in upper-class portrayals of masculinity, or as physical strength in working-class portrayals) can be accounted for by the impact of other discursive constructions, such as those pertaining to social class and ethnicity.

Hence I interpret the various 'kinds' of masculinity and femininity listed by such authors rather as the various ways in which men/boys attempt to achieve masculinity or femininity. In other words there are different strategies for constructing oneself as masculine or feminine, rather than different types of masculinity or femininity. This is particularly clear in the case of 'subjugated masculinities' (Connell, 1995). Gay men and South Asian boys are two groups often listed in works on 'masculinites' as illustrating 'subjugated masculinity' (types of masculinity apparently derided by 'hegemonic masculinity'). However, it is clear that there are different constructions among individuals within these groups (for example there are some very 'macho' gay men and South Asian heterosexual men, besides apparently 'effeminate' individuals). But most importantly in terms of this argument, 'effeminate' men are not 'doing' a 'different (subjugated) type' of masculinity – rather, they are men who do not display sufficient masculine traits to be seen as adequately masculine by other people. They may be actively choosing to behave differently from other men, or they may construct themselves as masculine, but their construction as 'not properly masculine' by others is due to their apparent *lack* of masculinity rather than 'different' masculinity. Thus they are constructed as 'other', like women (Walkerdine, 1990; Jordan, 1995), and hence are subjugated.

This raises the point that men and women may often display traits traditionally assigned to the opposite sex. Although the adoption of such behaviour risks being assigned to the 'other' and subsequent possible marginalization or rejection (Walkerdine, 1990; Davies, 1989), it may actually be (re)constructed as gender appropriate. For example, a woman might behave in competitive and aggressive ways, but her behaviour might be constructed as 'manipulative' or 'bitchy', stereotypically feminine characteristics. In my previous work (1998a,c), I have highlighted the extent to which the gender dichotomy can incorporate contradiction without disruption. In criticising some researchers' apparently contradictory conceptions of gender, where gender is conflated with sex, MacInnes (1998) asks why, if for example a woman is competitive and aggressive, she is not labelled masculine in research (where a man in her place would be). Thus he raises an extremely valuable but challenging point in asking why it is apparently only *boys* who choose masculinity and *girls* who choose femininity.

Can women be 'masculine' and men be 'feminine'? If these are purely social constructions, then logically the answer must be 'yes'. However, when we consider this, MacInnes's point proves edifying because it feels uncomfortable and stereotyping to label certain behaviour in a woman 'masculine' and certain behaviour in a man 'feminine'. This is partly because of the stigma attached to these terms when applied to the opposite sex (the labels are often deemed offensive when applied to the opposite sex, I would argue precisely because the application suggests that that individual has 'failed' at gender, and might therefore be marginalized). So instead people tend to reconstruct a woman's aggression as being manipulation, bitchiness or similar, which fits in with the dominant construction of femininity. Yet, if the terms 'masculinity' and 'femininity' cannot be applied to both sexes, the inference is that gendered behaviour is indeed tied essentially to sex. Perhaps we need to develop a new terminology. In the meantime, it seems adequate to refer to the work by Davies (1989; 1993), myself and others, who point to the ways in which the dominant gender dualism means that gender becomes a cornerstone of people's identity. Hence children and adults take up and perform gender (masculinity/femininity), usually according to the expectations relating to their biologically assigned sex. As Whitehead (1999) argues, masculinity is the discursive framework that men inhabit (and femininity the discursive framework that women inhabit). Therefore, when looking at gender constructions and identity in this book, my focus is the strategies and methods by which young people attempt to perform their gender, and any apparent changes, inconsistencies or resistance to these practices.

Returning to the issue of analysis of gender and other aspects of identity, Cealey Harrison and Hood-Williams (1998) have pointed out that the various structural differences affecting identity are so complex that it becomes impossible to analyse them all. They criticize notions of 'intersections' of aspects of identity such as race and gender, arguing that these factors do not 'intersect'; rather, they are entirely intermeshed and thus inseparable. Cealey Harrison and Hood-Williams conclude, however, that it is also pointless to attempt to analyse one factor (such as gender) when all the other factors are also affecting an individual's identity. Although not being able to answer these points completely, I would argue that to abandon such analysis would be to give up attempting to identify and act upon the very real continuing inequalities in our society. Thus I proceed with my analysis of gender, while recognizing that it is only one factor among many affecting the identity and behaviour of young people.

Some writers have queried the preoccupation of researchers with gender difference. For example, MacInnes (1998) maintains that the social construction of gender is simply an archaic leftover from a long-dead patriarchy (patriarchy having been killed off by the combined forces of contraception and capitalism, according to MacInnes). Yet I would respond that it is clearly the case that gender continues to affect our lives. One only has to enter school classrooms to see that, rather than having faded out among the younger generation, gender difference remains solidly entrenched in the interaction and social constructions of the next generation. One of the points I hope to emphasize in this book is how the oppositional construction of gender continues to invest power and agency in the male and devalues and subjugates the female. As a small example of how normalized these values remain in our society, I was recently struck by a billboard advertisement for a holiday company. To the right of a picture of a small white boy wearing swimming trunks and carrying a bucket ran the text:

Name:	Angus Fowler
Age:	7
Likes:	Helicopters, holidays, cameras
Dislikes:	Girls

Below this was the name of the holiday company and the caption, 'You are not a number'. Imagine if instead of 'Dislikes: Girls' it had read 'Dislikes: Black people', or some such! This is not to detract from the fact of continuing racism in British society but to illustrate the way in which even in these supposedly overpolitically correct times misogyny can be found amusing, normal ('all part of growing up', or 'boys will be boys') and even cute. Of course, one might argue that part of the humour in the advert is the irony that this (surely red-blooded, heterosexual) boy will doubtless change his mind about girls once he reaches puberty. Yet here again we confront the same spectre of misogyny: it is only when he becomes sexually active that girls can be seen to have value, in potentially meeting his sexual needs (see Holland et al. (1998) for an account of the ways in which heterosexual relations among young people locate power in the male).

Thus, although the lifestyles and expectations of men and women have certainly changed, the construction of gender difference, and many of the discourses, values, and inequalities on which these constructions are based, remain firmly ingrained. In this book I hope to show the ways in which some of these discourses and inequalities are perpetuated, and the ways in which they are (or might be) resisted.

The Theoretical Perspective behind the Study

The theoretical rationale for my approach to the research was largely developed from my previous research into gender constructions and power in primary school children.[2] My perspective is a social constructionist and feminist one. There are many different types of feminism. My feminist position is that gender difference is socially produced and often limiting to both sexes. Moreover, this social construction of gender difference holds important consequences in terms of power, because in the dichotomous construction of gender, power is located in the male, and the female is subjugated. I recognize that women's and men's experiences and access to power are by no means monolithic and that other factors such as social class, ethnicity, sexuality, and (dis)ability create important differences in the relative power of individual women and men. However, I also believe that the construction of gender difference leads women to share certain experiences, because of the almost universal subjugation of women and the feminine compared with men. As a feminist I believe that this situation is wrong, and that we should work to change it (Francis, 1998a; 1999b).

Social constructionists see meaning as being made through interaction with others. Since the 1980s, social constructionism has been influenced by post-structuralism and post-modernism (Burr, 1995). These positions suggest that the self is not a coherent and fixed personality, but rather is positioned and repositioned through 'discourses'. The term 'discourse' came to prominence in the social sciences via the influential work of Foucault. It refers to patterns of language or text that describe and position people and things in different ways. The example I always give is that of a housewife: she might be positioned as a victim of oppression in some types of feminist discourse, or as an idyllic example of a woman fulfilling her natural role in some types of conservative discourse. The main point about discourses is that they carry power in their ability to position things and people as negative or positive, powerless or powerful.

In applying this theoretical position to gender, gender is seen not as fixed but as socially constructed through various gender discourses (Francis, 1999b). Davies (1989) argues that dominant discursive practices position all subjects (and often objects) as being either male or female. Because these categories are relational ('man' can only exist in relation to what it is not – 'woman'), and are inherent to our construction of a social identity, apparent behavioural expressions of sex are taken up to demonstrate one's sex: this social construction of sex is what we term 'gender'. However, these constructions also bear consequences in terms of power, as in the gender dualism (or 'gender dichotomy', as I call it, see Francis, 1998a) power is assigned to the masculine. Davies (1989) maintains that women are only positioned as powerful in the domestic sphere, or by helping men. My research in primary school went further, showing that even in helping males, females abdicated power and were often marginalized as a result (Francis, 1997a; 1998a).

From this perspective, the task of the feminist is to identify and analyse the various gender discourses, so that these may be better understood and potentially deconstructed. I have become gradually disillusioned with post-structuralist positions, arguing that while useful for critique they are unable to (and even opposed to) contribute to the political, emancipatory work for change that a feminist position requires (see Francis, 1999b, for elaboration). Foucault (1992) maintained that the 'intellectual' should not tell people what to do, but should rather be a critic of existing practices. However, I would question whether it is more justifiable simply to ironically criticize social practices than to look for constructive solutions and recommend suggestions for change. I also question the assumption of the 'death of the coherent self' embedded in post-structuralist theory: some aspects of our individual characters appear to remain constant, despite other aspects altering, depending on the discursive environment or over time. Finally, I now feel that whereas power is often discursively produced, discourse is not power's only medium. Economic and physical power can also have a very real impact on people's lives. Exercises of physical or economic power are very often discursively explained or justified, yet it seems to me that these forms of power are worthy of analysis in their own right (see also Soper, 1990).

However, as my own research illustrates, the power of discourse remains an important area of exploration, especially in the field of gender. Hence I continue to believe that identifying and analysing the various discourses that are drawn upon in the construction of gender is a necessary facet of feminist research, even if this analysis of discourse is conducted in a feminist (and thus modernist[3]) endeavour. Therefore throughout the book the various ways in which gender is constructed by pupils in the classroom are explored, and sometimes the discourses that they appeared to drawn upon in their constructions are analysed. However, rather than simply pointing out these discursive practices in a critical manner, I also see it as an integral part of the feminist project that suggestions are made for ways in which we might disrupt and reconstruct these practices. I hope that by exploring the various gender discourses available to secondary school pupils, and the ways in which these discourses position males and females, we might be able to identify strategies for change. For a detailed discussion of my methods of discourse identification and analysis, see Francis (1999c).

Methods

The study described in this book was funded by the Economic and Social Research Council, and it involved research in three different secondary schools during the school year 1998–9. This work was conducted by me. A combination of methods were adopted. Classroom observation was used to record the classroom interaction and pupil behaviour during lessons. Individual interviews were used to ask pupils directly about gender issues in the classroom, gender and learning, and the pupils post-compulsory education and career plans.

The combination of research methods has traditionally been used for the purposes of triangulation (Smaling, 1993). However, my previous work demonstrates how young people often construct themselves and their opinions differently depending on the interactive environment (for instance when they are with friends, or when they are with an adult teacher or academic). I therefore expected some lack of consistency in terms of the subject positions adopted, but aimed to explore such diverse subject positions as well as any consistency in constructions of gender. Moreover, I aimed to use the observation to witness gendered classroom interaction first hand, and the subsequent interviews to ask the young people their opinions and interpretations of that interaction.

Sample

All three schools in which the research was conducted are located in London, representing inner-city (London underground zone 2), semi-suburban (zone 3) and greater London (zone 4) areas. The schools' populations represent various social classes and ethnic mixes; however, the majority of pupils in each school are from working-class backgrounds. Sandyfields Comprehensive School is situated in an inner-city area, surrounded by council estates. The majority of the pupils at the school are from ethnic minority groups, of whom the majority are Afro-Caribbean. The school also has an unusually high number of East Asian (particularly Vietnamese) pupils. Boys outnumber girls at the school by almost two to one, because there are a number of single-sex girls' schools in the catchment area. Yet girls still outperform boys at the school. In 1998, only seventeen pupils achieved five or more 'C' grades at GCSE, of whom two-thirds were girls. Sandyfields School came second from bottom in its area league table in 1999.

Table 2.1 Ethnicity and gender in the total interview sample

Gender	Anglo		Afro-Caribbean		South Asian		East Asian		Mixed race		African		Mediterranean		South American		Middle Eastern	
	F	M	F	M	F	M	F	M	F	M	F	M	F	M	F	M	F	M
Number	18	15	10	22	7	2	6	1	4	3	0	6	2	1	2	0	1	0
Total (n = 100)	33		32		9		7		7		6		3		2		1	

Table 2.2 Classroom observation

School	Year	Set	Subject
Sandyfields	11	Middle	Maths
	11	Top	English
	10	Middle	English
	10	Top	Maths
St Mark's	11	Middle	Maths
	11	Middle	English
	10	Top	English
	10	Top	Maths
Richardson	11	Top	Maths
	11	Middle	English
	10	Middle	Maths
	10	Top	English

were observed in all, and for each class a lesson was observed three times. Table 2.2 shows the various classes observed.

Classroom Observation

Staff were informed about the aims of the research project, and pupils were told that the researcher was interested in their classroom interaction and in their opinions on a number issues (which would become evident in the interviews). The limited information given to respondents raises the issue of empowerment and the 'informed consent' of respondents when agreeing to participate in the research (see Robson, 1993). It could be argued that a lack of detailed explanation about the issues I was studying maintained the dichotomy of the knowing/powerful researcher and the unaware, powerless researched, which feminist researchers have traditionally attempted to minimize (see, for example, Skeggs, 1994; Stanley and Wise, 1993). On the other hand, as Stanley and Wise (1993) and Denscombe (1995) observe, the researcher chooses the subject of the research, the methodology, usually most of the methods and the practical issues (such as time taken, sample, etc.) around them, and has most control over data analysis and dissemination. This means that even in 'emancipatory research' where efforts are made to empower respondents within the research process, a power dichotomy inevitably exists between the researcher and the researched.

In terms of the classroom observation, I was simply and openly observing the behaviour of the young people. It was important that I did not provide too much detail about the issues my research examined, for fear that this knowledge would impact upon and alter the participants' gendered behaviour in the classroom. On the other hand, it is also recognized that the researcher's presence inevitably affects the interaction taking place, and that consequently the observer plays an integral part in the interaction (Francis, 1998a; Carspecken, 1996).

In the classroom many interactions occur at once, and much of the interaction is subtle and extremely complex (Wragg, 1994; Carspecken, 1996). In some classes the majority of the pupils were talking almost constantly. Therefore, I was quite aware that the speech recorded by my written observation notes is only a fragment of the total classroom talk, and often particularly represents the tables nearest to me (it was sometimes impossible to hear what was going on at other tables because of the general noise level). Following Carspecken (1996), I used both note-taking and audio-taping in classroom observation. The notes made in the classroom could then be cross-referenced with the audio-tape for triangulation to check my interpretations, and to add more information. Taping the classroom interaction tackled the problem, to some extent, of hearing the talk of some pupils at the expense of other pupils (though not completely). A looser journal was also kept to record observations and conversations on the school site outside the classroom: this contained 'on-the-spot' observations. I always attempted to make notes in this notebook as soon as possible after the events took place. Efforts were also made that the fieldwork notes be put on to a word processor as soon as possible after recording took place, in order to reduce the risk of misinterpretation due to lack of memory of events.

It is recognized that the longer a researcher spends in a particular environment, the less impact they have on the interaction taking place (the participants become accustomed to the presence of the researcher; see Carspecken, 1996). Each class involved had three lessons observed, which is admittedly not a long time. My options concerning the periods spent in classrooms were restricted by time. The intention was to conduct a broad-scale study in a relatively short space of time. Therefore, I felt that covering a large sample of pupils in a number of different schools was more important than spending a longer amount of time with a smaller sample. The interviews were used to probe the pupils' constructions more deeply. However, the limited amount of time spent observing each class is one of the limitations in my approach. Certainly, it could not be claimed that I immersed myself in a particular classroom, as with traditional ethnographic research in schools.

Indeed, while taking my observation notes in the classroom, I became increasingly relieved that I had not attempted a study of the children's specific learning styles. In a class of over thirty children, interaction is incredibly complex. Much of it is non-verbal (what Edwards and Westgate (1994) refer to as 'silent language') and extremely subtle. A tape recorder cannot pick up this interaction, and inevitably a single observer will miss a great deal of it. I realized that by giving attention to certain aspects of interaction (for instance the number and gender of children asking the teacher questions and the types of response given) the observer misses others (for example the numbers and genders of children working co-operatively in groups). Just as the teacher is forced to give more attention to loud or disruptive pupils, so the researcher tends to record the actions of such pupils more frequently than others. This is partly because such pupils draw more attention to themselves, and partly because, whatever their intentions, researchers tend to be drawn to material that they deem to be exciting or controversial.

Very little has been written concerning the experience and feelings of the classroom observer when conducting this type of research. Even in feminist classroom observational studies, such as Spender's (1982) and Stanworth's (1981) classic studies of gendered interaction, the researcher's own presence and experience of the research process is largely absent in the reports. This was the first time I had been an observer in a secondary school classroom, and I initially found that taking my place at the back or front of the classroom was an embarrassing and threatening experience. I remembered how we pupils had treated observers during my own school days. As a result I felt very vulnerable and consequently quite nervous. I expected to hear personal comments about me being loudly whispered, rubbers to hit me on the head and tampons to fly into my lap. In fact, I was amazed how little attention pupils gave me in the classroom. Some asked me if I was an inspector, and this may provide a clue to the pupils' apparent acceptance at being observed: observation by inspectors and the like is more common now than when I was at school during the 1980s. However, albeit thirteen years since I did my 'O' levels (I was in the last cohort to do 'O' levels before GCSEs were introduced), I was initially overwhelmed with feelings of familiarity and *déjà vu* when beginning my observation in secondary school, and this was particularly the case in Richardson school, which of the three schools was the most like my old comprehensive in terms of the social class and ethnic make-up of the pupil population. As someone who had not previously taught in secondary school, it felt initially peculiar to enter the classroom as an adult and led me to question my own identity as an observer.

Teachers also responded to my presence in class in different ways. One male teacher used me as a disciplinary tool, saying to a girl who was messing about with a boy at the back of the class (with a sideways look at me), "do you know you're being observed?" Some were clearly concerned that I was observing their teaching practice as well as the pupils' behaviour. The presence of the researcher can cause teachers to reflect on their practice more than usual. For example, my notes record:

9.45 a.m.   I enter class with a couple of students. Ms D is still telling off a
boy from the last class
Ms D: You'll come back and see me at break
Boy: I *ain't*, I ain't coming back at all {Those boys exit and more
           pupils enter}
           (Observer comment: Ms D looks tired)
Ms D: {to me} I'm glad you weren't here for the last one [lesson]

In this sense, it seems important that the researcher bears in mind that their presence as an observer can feel threatening or intimidating to the teacher, and constitute an extra pressure in an already highly pressurized job. So where possible the researcher should try to put teachers at ease.

Interviews

After the observation period, I handed out letters to parents asking whether they objected to their sons/daughters being interviewed. I then selected a random sample of pupils whose parents had not objected and who did not object themselves. Four girls and four boys were drawn from each of the classes (thus eight pupils from four classes at each school). An extra two girls and two boys were chosen, bringing the total interview sample to 100 pupils (fifty girls and fifty boys). The interviews were usually of 15–20 minutes' duration, and were audio-recorded. It was made clear in the interviews that the respondents could leave questions unanswered if they wanted. The interviews were semi-structured, based around a list of core questions. For a list of these questions, see Appendix 1. For an outline of the transcript conventions, see Appendix 2. Pseudonyms have been provided for all participants.

A number of issues were raised during the interviews with secondary school pupils. It was the first time I had interviewed young people from the 14- to 16-year-old age group, and one of the first things that struck me was how initially uneasy and monosyllabic many of the boys were in an individual interview situation compared with their counterparts in primary or post-compulsory education. Of course, there were many exceptions: a number of the boys were extremely articulate, and many came to the interviews obviously relishing the opportunity to talk. Moreover, a small number of girls also appeared awkward or withdrawn in the interviews. Yet such awkwardness was far more common in boys. This may in part have been due to my gender. However, I got the impression that some boys simply were not used to talking, and that they felt uncomfortable in a one to one, apparently serious, discussion. As a result, my research notebook records my concern:

I am taking quite a winsome, warm/jokey approach, and using a lot of slang, in order to relax them [boys] and make them feel comfortable. However, this may result in a particularly 'playful' interview. Does seem necessary to get them talking, though.

(Interview notes)

This strategy did seem to work in terms of making the boys feel more at ease and 'getting them talking'. However, it also raises uncomfortable issues of heterosexual gender relations: the way in which a female interviewer accommodates boys and works (in quite a gendered way) to make them feel comfortable, whereas the co-operation of girls tends to be taken for granted.

Conversely, there were times when I felt that by laughing conspiratorially or nodding at girls' derogatory comments about 'the boys' and 'men' I was colluding with them in a sexist construction. Pattman et al. (1998a) have also discussed Pattman's similar feelings of discomfort when boys talked of 'the girls' in sexist and misogynist terms, and how he felt that his presence in this talk and lack of protest at it made him culpable in it.

A further problematic issue raised in the interviews was that of confidentiality. In an interview with Monica, she complained that some of the boys in her language class were sexually harassing her, by continually groping and verbally abusing her. When I suggested that she complain to her teacher and to her head of year, she told me that she had already complained on numerous occasions, and that the boys had been disciplined (inadequately, according to Monica), but that despite this the harassment was continuing. This left me in a similar predicament to the time when a primary school boy complained of bullying in his interview (Francis, 1998a). Although I would argue as a feminist that one is obliged to act in these situations, it can feel uncomfortable raising 'problems' and apparently interfering in the school that has done you the favour of allowing access. Teachers can feel suspicious and defensive around researchers, particularly in light of the expert academic/ignorant practitioner hierarchy, which it has been suggested is evoked by much educational research (Shkedi, 1998). In this case I reported Monica's complaint of on-going sexual harassment to her head of year. Her response demonstrates the complexity of these issues, as she said that contrary to Monica's claim she had received no previous complaints of harassment from Monica. However, she said she was glad I had told her, and indicated that she would make further inquiries.

This chapter has outlined the theoretical perspective and methods used in the study. The following chapters will discuss the data produced by the study concerning young people's gender constructions in the secondary school classroom.

3 Gendered Classroom Culture

Background

There is a large body of feminist work based on the observation of gendered interaction in the classroom. This work has catalogued the different forms of behaviour among boys and girls at school, the gendered ways in which teachers interact with pupils and one another, and the ways in which the very culture of the school perpetuates gender difference. On entering the secondary classroom, it is immediately noticeable that where pupils have been allowed to choose their own seating, boys usually sit next to boys and girls next to girls. Adler and Adler (1998) have observed that the sexes tend to segregate between the mid-primary and early secondary school ages, but begin to interact more in the late 'pre-adolescent' years. However, it is important to point out that this interaction is by no means total: friendship groups often remain exclusively single-sex, and interaction between girls and boys is often limited to talk and banter across the classroom.

The readily observable tendencies of differences in pupil behaviour according to gender has led some researchers to refer to 'gender cultures' in school. Thorne (1993) has criticized this term, arguing that it is typically used in psychological research in education and indicates assumptions of gender essentialism – the idea that boys and girls are inherently different and that this therefore manifests in separate gender cultures. However, I have argued elsewhere (1998a) that the notion of symbolic gender cultures can encapsulate the worked-upon, polarized and perpetuated difference in gender constructions among pupils in school. This chapter analyses some of the findings from my classroom observation. It explores the various factors that contributed to, or were used by pupils to perpetuate, the construction of gender difference in the secondary school classroom.

Gendered Classroom Behaviour

Some of the most obvious differences in classroom behaviour according to gender are the ways in which boys tend to monopolize space in the classroom and playground, and the ways in which girls tend to draw less attention to themselves than do boys (Spender, 1982; Whyte, 1986; Davies, 1989; Thorne, 1993). Howe (1997) and Younger et al. (1999) found that boys dominate the classroom vocally too, making more noise and more frequent contributions during whole-class teaching than did girls. Younger et al. found that boys asked more questions and were asked more questions by teachers. My findings confirm this. And in all three schools in which I conducted observation, boys moved around in the classroom and were more physically active than girls. They frequently kicked balls around, walked or ran around the classroom, pushed, slapped or hit each other, and threw things across the class. Girls sometimes walked about in class, but less frequently than did boys, and they rarely engaged in any of the other physical activities listed above in class. Moreover, in eight of the twelve classes I observed, boys were substantially noisier than girls, both in terms of general noise among pupils and in terms of contributions during whole-class teaching.

Of course, it is important to point out that not all boys were engaged in noisy or physical behaviour in the classroom, and that in two of the classes observed groups of girls made the most noise. (In the remaining two classes girls and boys tended to be equally noisy.) This illustrates the tendency towards overgeneralization that is involved with analysing young people solely in terms of gender, as discussed in Chapter 2. I shall try to maintain an awareness of this point throughout the discussion of the data, drawing attention to resistance to gender norms and to atypical constructions of gender as well as to the dominant constructions of gender in the classroom.

The next section discusses teachers' gendered responses to pupils. The remainder of the chapter catalogues and explores the various ways in which pupils constructed their gender identities and perpetuated gender differences in the classroom.

The Teachers' Constructions of Gender

The teacher's perceptions of gender differences and their consequent interaction with, and expectations of, pupils, have been shown to affect classroom interaction and pupil self-perception.[1] However, research has found that since the 1980s many teachers are now more aware of, and sensitive to, gender issues than had previously been the case (Kenway et al., 1994; Arnot et al., 1999). Moreover, as was pointed out in the first chapter, the pattern of gendered achievement at secondary school level has altered, with girls equalling or outperforming boys in virtually all subjects at GCSE level. It might be expected that knowledge of this might impact on teachers' expectations of pupils. Indeed, at Sandyfields School some pupils reported that their (female) teacher had told them about girls' outperformance of boys. However, at St Mark's School pupils reported that their (female) teacher had declared that boys tended to be better at figures and girls better at languages, showing that traditional perceptions persist. Moreover, teachers could often promote gender stereotypes and perpetuate the gender divide in more subtle ways: an example is when Ms D told a boy to take his hat off, saying, "You're in the presence of ladies". Another is the way in which an English teacher generated class laughter and embarrassed a boy by allocating him a female part to read during a play reading. (It could be argued that this latter action breaks down gender barriers by ignoring sex-appropriate allocation, but in fact it strengthened the gender polarity by positioning the boy as ridiculous in having to play a girl's part. Indeed, the boy's embarrassment confirmed the rigidity of the gender duality by highlighting the consequences of transgression.)

The teachers' knowledge of gender issues was occasionally reflected in their interaction with me. The teachers had been told of the focus of my research, and it is possible that their knowledge of my interest affected the classroom interaction. One teacher whispered comments to me on the gender relations in her class a number of times as I was observing. In another class, in which boys almost always responded to the teacher's questions to the class while girls took a 'back seat', the teacher said at one point that she wanted a girl to answer, because "the girls are getting lazy". She met my eye as she made this comment, leading me to wonder whether her decision to ask "the girls" for an answer was influenced by my presence.

Some teachers did appear to respond to boys and girls differently in the classroom. In discussing this it is of course important to remember that, as I have already pointed out, the behaviour of pupils in secondary schools is strongly gendered, to the extent that it becomes possible to talk of symbolic gender cultures. In this sense, it is hardly surprising that teachers tend to talk about or to 'the girls' or 'the boys' in class, or even relate to pupils differently depending on their gender. Hence the perpetuation of the gender polarization may be circular.

In Chapter 5 I discuss the reports of some boys that teachers are more lenient with girls than they are with boys. The concerns of boys about this have been noted elsewhere (Younger and Warrington, 1996; Pickering, 1997; Skelton, 1997; Phoenix et al., forthcoming). I recorded a number of incidents that seemed to confirm this view. On one occasion, two boys were told to sit down, when a girl with them was also standing. Boys were sometimes told off for making a noise or failing to concentrate, when girls were continuing to whisper together. However, this may be related to the point that boys tended to be noisier in the classroom. Younger et al. (1999) found that boys were more frequently disciplined than girls, but note that it is difficult to ascertain whether or not this was justified by the boys' behaviour. Because many boys tend to be so loud, the teacher may notice their talk more, or the need to quieten them may be more immediate than in the case of girls (as their greater volume causes more disruption to the class). It was certainly the case that during the observation I tended to learn the boys' names more quickly than the girls' because the boys' names were used more often by the teacher.

Moreover, two of the male teachers appeared to take a different approach to the girls and the boys. Mr L took a very challenging style with the more confident boys in his maths class, frequently putting them on the spot and using sarcasm. Many boys appeared to relish this: the majority of boys in the class were extremely vocal, regularly and enthusiastically shouting out answers, whereas the girls were much less vocal and rarely volunteered answers. In turn, Mr L was far more sympathetic and kind to the girls, and he was more tolerant of any lack of understanding. This may have been because he did not want to intimidate them, but it had the effect of allowing girls to refrain from participation. A number of girls in this class sat at the back of the classroom and were observed regularly chatting together about other subjects while the pupils (mainly boys) at the front of the class were completely engrossed in the maths problems. Mr L's different approach with them also seemed to be sensed by some of the girls, who 'played up' to him. For example, Mr L is helping Clara and Leticia at their table:

Clara (To Mr L):   See I'm really clever now ain't I?
Mr L: You're *wonderful* {he moves to the next table}.

Such slightly flirtatious banter and difference in approach to girls on the part of male teachers has been discussed by Skelton (2000) in her work in the primary school. She argues that heterosexuality underpins the classroom management of pupils and draws on discourses that allow ideological and structural domination of some groups over others.

As with Mr L's approach to the boys, Mr Q had an extremely abrasive classroom manner, and he frequently used sarcasm or shouted at pupils. For example, Rick (an Afro-Caribbean boy who presents himself as 'hard') asks Mr Q a question, suggesting an interpretation and asking if he is on the right track. Mr Q responds,

Mr Q: *Duuuuuuhhh* (.) it's not about *sound*, [it's about=
Rick: [I won't have any
        confidence if you go 'duuhhh' all the time
Mr Q: {laughs} It'd take a lot to destroy *your* confidence, pal

invest power in the male, and also to be properly masculine one must be heterosexually active), gay men are positioned as being non-masculine and other. For example, the pupils on Claudine's table were discussing someone they believed to be 'gay', and Claudine agrees, he "looks like a girl". To Claudine, the person's looking like a girl appears to suggest his lack of 'proper' masculine behaviour in terms of his sexuality. Because gay men are constructed as lacking masculinity (and thus 'like females'), their very existence poses a threat to the dominant construction of masculinity as powerful via active heterosexual relations. It is no surprise, then, that in a school culture which promotes traditional constructions of compulsory and male-dominated heterosexuality, homophobia is rife.

To be called gay (for example 'battyman', 'queer', 'poof', 'fag') was a common form of abuse in the schools. Such homophobia was not restricted to the pupils: in one staffroom a female teacher said of a new member of staff, "He's got a very weak handshake – he'll have to improve in my opinion". Her female colleague agreed, "I'm thinking what you're thinking".

It appeared that to position another pupil as gay, either in a jokey or serious manner, could provide a demonstration of a boy's own heterosexuality and thus increase the security of his construction of masculinity. An example is provided by the following classroom interaction between Wayne (Anglo) and David (Afro-Caribbean), who sit together in a maths class:

Wayne: David, stop distracting me
David: {mock humble} Sorry Wayne
Wayne: You *will* be (.) David, stop tryin'a play footsie gay boy {David laughs} [...]
Wayne: {shouting at David} Eeuur, leave my leg alone (.) eeuur, gay boy, David, get your hand off my leg!
            Ms W sends Wayne out of the room. He doesn't move
David: {to Wayne} *You're* gay man, you're such a poof (.) if I put my hand on your leg why haven't you moved? (.) get up man {Ms W shouts at Wayne, insisting he leave the room. Wayne exits}.

Homophobia is a major form of bullying in schools (Skelton, 1997). Salisbury and Jackson (1996) and Mac an Ghaill (1999) maintain that homophobic abuse actually constitutes a form of sexual harassment. Salisbury and Jackson (1996) dramatically portray the lengths boys will go to in order to avoid being branded 'queer', arguing that, "boys must be seen to be openly, obviously and even rampantly heterosexual. Any sign of 'deviant' behaviour will be pounced on by the pack who are your friends" (p. 168.) Again, this reminds us how sexuality is mutually constructed and policed by pupils. Following from his argument that young men are being sexually harassed via homophobic abuse, Mac an Ghaill (1999) maintains that writing on sexual harassment has been too preoccupied with gender. However, this seems to miss the point that such harassment is linked to the positioning of gay men as 'other' and like women. In this sense, homophobia is closely linked to misogyny.

Hence the denigration of the non-masculine, which is reflected in homophobia, also extends to the denigration of girls and women. Besides the objectification of girls discussed under 'Homophobia and mysogny', this misogyny was reflected in the terms of abuse and insults constantly in use in and outside the classroom. Lees (1993) has discussed the way in which the majority of terms of abuse relate to women or to female bodily parts, reflecting social practices of regulation and surveillance of women as well as contempt for things female. She discusses how words denoting female genitalia such as 'cunt' and 'twat' are seen as more severe forms of abuse than those denoting male genitalia (e.g. 'prick', 'dickhead'), presumably reflecting revulsion and contempt for female genitalia. However, a relatively new development appears to be the use of words such as 'pussy' as a term of abuse among males. Rather than suggesting someone who has been mean (e.g. 'cunt') or stupid ('twat'), 'pussy' is used to suggest that a male is a 'wimp'/non-masculine, besides referring to female genitalia. Hence the reference to female genitalia in this term itself appears to denote a lack of masculinity. Moreover, I found many examples of boys using terms of abuse previously applied to females against other males: for example, 'bitch'. The use of such terms against other males implies a 'double whammy' in that the term not only implies a lack of masculinity in its evocation of a woman, but it also implies a denigrated woman. There was also much abuse of mothers in pupils' insults. Examples include 'your mum's a whore', 'your mum's a ho' and 'motherfucker'. So misogyny and homophobia are both reflected in secondary school pupils' terms of abuse (particularly those of boys).

Salisbury and Jackson (1996) show how use of such language helps to bind boys together as well as (or by) displaying hostility to things female. Sexist jokes and misogynist abuse help to sustain the gender order, positioning the male as superior.

Verbal and Physical Aggression

Such verbal abuse was far more common among boys than among girls, reflecting the bantering, but very often confrontational and aggressive, ways in which boys talk to one another. It could also sometimes be applied to teachers: I have already discussed the very confrontational style adopted by

Mr Q in class, and one boy in particular, Rick, reacted with a similar style of his own. He frequently attempted to assert himself against Mr Q, and my observation notes record a number of occasions when he surreptitiously abused Mr Q; for example, pulling an aggressive face at Mr Q's back, and leaning forward and mouthing "you fuck, you fuck" at him. I have already discussed how boys were far more physically active in the classroom than were girls. This activity often included hitting or kicking one another (playfully or otherwise), throwing things at one another, or whipping one another with scarves and the like. There were many instances when boys threatened one another with violence. For example:

Shofic:	{to Justice} Shut up[4] or I'll beat the fuck out of you
Raymond:	{loudly to another boy} Fuck you man
Mr U:	*Raymond* (.) *Raymond* (.) I don't know how many times I've told you (.) I don't mind you and Justice working together, but turn around and face the *front* of the *room*
Shofic:	{to Raymond} Ah *shut up* man
Raymond:	{to Justice} Don't argue or I'll break you

Rakeem:	I don't understand (.) how'm I meant to know what to do?
Clive:	*Shut* up
Rakeem:	(3) I don't know what to do (.) {Clive says something and Rakeem retorts} You don't know yourself (2) how'm I gonna know what to do? (.) {to Clive} do you smoke? (.) do you smoke?
Clive:	*[.] you fuck [.]* {he raises his fist at Rakeem, who cowers good-humouredly}

Of course, while the boys concerned only threaten violence, this interaction reflects competition among boys in their struggle to construct themselves as masculine by demonstrating their physical strength and power at the expense of other boys. Dixon (1996) and Skelton (1999) point out that maintenance of a construction of aggressive and competitive masculinity involves constant confrontation and challenges between boys. Hence their 'jokey' punches, raised fists, kicks and headlocks similarly portray the delineation of a masculine 'hardness' hierarchy, where acknowledged 'hard' boys such as Clive remind other boys of their power and prestige, and less evidently hard boys such as Raymond and Justice compete for pre-eminence and for a higher or more secure place in the hierarchy. In this sense, as Skelton (1999) observes, it is extremely important that boys avoid showing any sign of hurt or weakness. The most common way to pass off such violent or potentially violent behaviour was via humour, in the form of laughingly ignoring or distracting the other boy, or in humorous deference, as in the example of Rakeem and Clive.

I did not observe any examples of girls hitting or kicking each other in class, nor any instances of boys hitting or kicking girls. However, there were two occasions where the possibility of male violence against girls was raised. In the first, Denzel (Afro-Caribbean) and Catrina (Anglo) were table mates in a maths class and were very competitive concerning their work (this was usually evident from Denzel's shouted comments that he was either ahead of, or catching up with, Catrina). On one occasion Denzel grabbed his bag and moved onto the next table in an apparent temper. Catrina laughed at him and said "Can't take the pace". He retorted angrily, "Nah, I just don't wanna *hurt* you". In this sense he presented himself as removing himself from the temptation of physically punishing Catrina, simultaneously reminding her (and himself) of his physical strength, and that he could overpower her physically if he so wished (even if not mentally).

In the second example, Alan made fun of a school play that Felicity had been involved in, and Felicity responded by attempting to position herself in an unamused teacher role, disciplining Alan. However, Alan was unwilling to be so positioned:

Alan: Yeh (.) […] fell asleep in your own rehearsal (.) {laughs}
Felicity: (.) I don't find that funny (.) now put your head down and work
Alan: {low, measured voice} Felicity after the lesson you and me are gonna fight (.)
Felicity: (.) *Scary*!
            (Observer comment: there is almost total silence in class as this is said – tension. There is a pause before chat resumes.)

The tense silence of the class was surprising. Perhaps the pupils were scared of Alan's (the largest boy in the class) anger and possible reaction, or perhaps they were waiting to see how Felicity (an assertive girl with an acid tongue) would respond. However, apparently sensing the tension and unwilling to risk escalation, Felicity retorts "scary!" sarcastically and resumes her work, her remark tempered to save her own face but sufficiently mild to avoid further confrontation. Significantly, both these examples show instances when a girl appeared to be challenging a boy. In doing so, the girl challenges the boy's masculinity (to be made to look silly, or 'bested', by a girl is clearly damaging to a construction of masculinity). Hence in response, both these examples demonstrate how boys could draw on their superior physical strength in order to discipline girls who appeared to pose a threat to their construction of masculinity, thus repositioning themselves as superior and powerful.

Use, or threatened use, of physical violence was not practised exclusively by boys, however. In one class a girl led discussions on how another girl had confronted her in the playground at break, and her plans to physically challenge the girl next breaktime. On another occasion words were exchanged between Claudine and Daniel, and she foolingly threatened him with a ruler, saying, "I'll cut your face if–". Such actions as Claudine's, though playful, hardly sit easily with traditional constructions of femininity. That some girls actually had the physical resources with which to reverse or ignore traditional gender constructions was dramatically illustrated to me in a corridor at Sandyfields School when the pupils were queuing up for lessons:

Notebook (19/10/98)
In the corridor while waiting for a teacher I see two girls hit boys, hard. Both girls are Afro-Caribbean, both boys white. The girls are much bigger than the boys concerned (they're about 13 years old). In one case, the girl hit the boy full in the face (I heard the sound), and it came up red straight away. He was restrained from retaliation by another Afro-Caribbean girl.

I was quite shocked by this incident, particularly as it raises issues about intergender violence. Boys are usually very conscious that they *should* not hit girls, because of girls' apparently lesser strength (Holland et al., 1998). Such regulatory discourse has not been applied to girls in relation to violence against boys. In the primary school I showed how physical bullying is practised by boys against boys and girls (1997b; 1998a). Yet this incident illustrates the potential of some girls, particularly in the early secondary school years when many girls are larger than boys, to physically bully boys. However, as such violence is in opposition to the dominant construction of femininity, it is likely to be rare.

Gendered Pastimes and Subjects of Talk

My research in primary schools showed how the pupils use talk about, and are interested in, particular gender-typed subjects to demonstrate their gender allegiance and to aid their construction of gender as relational. These practices were also evident in the secondary school. As in the primary school, one of the subjects boys used most frequently to construct their masculinity was football. Skelton (2000) found that even boys who did not seem to be good at football demonstrated a keen interest in it and presented themselves as good at football in their interviews with her. This illustrates the importance of appearing competent at practices and pastimes designated 'proper male pursuits'.

Talk about football punctuated boys' classroom interaction in all three secondary schools, although I recorded fewer occasions when football was mentioned at Sandyfields, possibly because boys seemed preoccupied with other pursuits (such as challenging the teacher). Certainly, boys did not play football less at Sandyfields; indeed, this school had the highest number of interviewees who reported playing for youth league teams in professional clubs. At all the schools, boys talked about football in couples and in large groups in the classroom. I noted discussions on favourite and national teams, playing football in school, football injuries and trips to watch matches.

As in Skelton's (2000) research, some teachers attempted to appeal to pupils by using football analogies to illustrate points. For example, when discussing war poems, Mr D attempted to draw an analogy between feeling compelled to fight in a war and the efforts to which one might go to secure tickets for the World Cup. Girls in the class pointed out that one could not justify killing for World Cup tickets, a point Mr D was forced to accede.

The only other topics that I noticed boys particularly discussing in all-male groups in the classroom were sexual activity (see pp. 36–39) and information technology. Computers and computer games were not discussed anywhere near the same extent as was football, but they were talked about by various boys. Indeed in one maths class four boys discussed computers and computer games throughout the lesson. It is interesting to note that it tended to be less physically 'hard' boys that discussed computers: I did not observe any of the 'hard' boys discussing this subject. This suggests the possibility that computers may be a masculine-typed pastime that boys perhaps less able to present themselves in a 'macho' manner can use to construct themselves as masculine.

Although they were constantly whispering to one another, it was far harder to ascertain the subject-matter of girls' conversations, because they tended to speak more quietly than boys. Some girls, often especially those who presented themselves in a particularly feminine manner, talked about subjects relating to appearance. I observed various girls talking about one another's hair, as well as brushing and putting up their hair. Mr Q delighted in spotting and ridiculing such expressions of a preoccupation with appearance:

Mr Q: Felicity (.) looking in the mirror is just going to frighten you for the rest of the lesson {Felicity and others laugh, and she draws away from the mirror}
Felicity gets up, collects her bags, goes to the wall mirror and applies her lip-salve
Mr Q: You don't get assessed on *appearance* Felicity

Of course, as Holland et al. point out (1998), appearance is expected to be a concern for girls, and many invest much time and effort in their grooming. Such grooming and control of the body in the form of dieting and the like is usually geared to achieving a 'look' that conforms to society's construction of the beautiful (slim, glamorous and curvaceous) woman (Francis, 1998a). It is also framed by the dominant construction of compulsory heterosexuality, where a woman must ensure she is attractive to men. Yet ironically, the research by Holland et al. (1998) shows that although young women are extremely concerned about their appearance and many are involved in the regulation of their bodies in the form of dieting and shaving, the majority are extremely ignorant concerning female bodily pleasure. Indeed, such an interest can be constructed as non-feminine.

I found myself despairing that Clara (Anglo) and Leticia (mixed race) spent so much of their English lesson discussing their hair, because their behaviour seemed to support the stereotypes of girls and their concerns being presented by some boys in their interviews (see Chapter 7, and also Pattman et al., 1999). However, on reflection I also considered the irony that in constructions of heterosexuality girls are expected to 'look nice' in order to please men, yet simultaneously male values despise such concerns with appearance, presenting them as evidence of female vanity and superficiality. Certainly it can be asked whether talk about appearance is any less worthwhile than talk about football; although it is the case that such constructions of femininity also serve to perpetuate dominant constructions of compulsory heterosexuality.

However, growing sales in menswear, perfumery, and men's health and fashion magazines demonstrate that men too are beginning to take renewed interest in their appearance. It may not be so acceptable for them to discuss aspects of appearance with their peers as it is for women, although market research has shown that some young men now go shopping for clothes in groups (an apparently new phenomenon). There were a number of comments in the classroom that reflected such male interest in appearance. For example, James makes fun of Anthony for having dandruff, and Andrew sings 'Salon Selectives' at him. Mr Q's witticisms were not only reserved for girls:

> *Alan leans back and adjusts his shirt in the mirror*
> Mr Q: *Alan, don't frighten yourself* {Alan laughs}.

Gendered Responses

A further way in which gender was performed in the classroom was via responses to various stimuli. Girls and boys responded differently according to their gender. One example concerns boys' apparent liking for violence.

For example, while reading *To Kill a Mocking Bird*, Ms X read the part about Boo stabbing his father's leg. Paul commented, "Should've stabbed 'im in the eye" (someone tuts). However, as Buckingham (1993) observes, this apparent enjoyment of violence should not be interpreted as an inherent tendency in boys, but rather as a means by which boys can demonstrate their masculinity.

A particularly interesting opportunity for me to analyse pupils' gendered responses arose when Ms N brought her baby (approximately 18 months old) in to her English lesson. Her child minder was ill and she had been unable to make alternative arrangements. She strapped the baby's hanging chair next to her at the front desk. Many of the girls in the class initially lavished gushing attention on the baby:

9.00 a.m.   *Natasha, Lisa, Sharon and a couple of other girls (about six in total) gather around the front desk cooing.*

9.04 a.m.   *Various girls ask Ms N what the baby's name is, and whether she'll be bringing her in next week.*
              Ms N tries to begin the task, telling them to turn to page 20.

Chloe: Same colour hair as you, has your husband got blond hair as well?

Ms N: Yeh

Sharon: Same colour eyes {Natasha and Sharon are sitting right next to the baby, looking at it adoringly}

However, my notes also include the observer comment, 'several boys are watching the baby, some with fond looks, some amused. They do seem interested, but are not vocal about it like some of the girls.' As the lesson developed, some of the girls who had been initially interested in the baby refocused their attention on their work, only looking at the baby when it made a noise. Yet some of the boys continued watching the baby attentively throughout the lesson. My notes record:

> *Chloe keeps looking across at the baby, which is playing with a pen.*
> *Ms N asks them to read again. Baby grabs at something, and a couple of girls chuckle. More boys are now watching the baby fondly/with interest than are girls.*
> *Natasha is playing with the baby.*

Ms N: Natasha concentrate please.
> *Aron and Thomas are looking at the baby fondly. Ms M explains about making puppet heads over Christmas.*

These extracts seem to suggest that while interest in the baby was evidenced in both girls and boys, girls were more likely to draw attention to this interest, arguably because such interest aids their construction of a 'proper femininity'. Although the baby held the attention of a number of boys, to vocalize such interest would have been potentially damaging to their construction of masculinity.

Discussion

In this chapter I have attempted to show the ways in which gender differences are performed and perpetuated in the classroom, creating an impression of different gender cultures. In these symbolic cultures boys are constructed as active, aggressive and competitive, and interested in particular pursuits such as football, heterosexual sexual conquest and information technology. Conversely, some girls used a preoccupation with appearance and stereotypically gendered responses to stimuli in order to position themselves as feminine. The resources which boys used to construct their masculinity tended to be more visible and obvious than those of the girls', simply because boys were more vocal and assertive. It was clear that girls were not simply passive, but they did not tend to assert their presence in the classroom in the same manner that the boys did (this is arguably an aspect of their construction of femininity, as we shall see in the next chapter).

I hope to have illustrated the ways in which overt heterosexuality and sexism, homophobia, misogyny, verbal and physical aggression, gendered pastimes and subjects of talk, and gendered responses could be used by pupils to demonstrate gender allegiance and to construct pupils' masculine or feminine identities. I have not yet discussed how learning and school orientation could apparently also be used in this way. Because the issue of gendered learning styles and boys' underachievement has recently become a particularly contested issue, this issue is examined by itself in Chapter 7. Likewise, the implications of pupils' gender constructions for their power and status in the classroom, and for their educational achievement, are discussed in later chapters.

There are two areas raised in this chapter that teachers may be able to influence directly. The first is the suggestion that some teachers interact differently with boys and girls, adopting a more robust, bantering style with boys and a more lenient, caring approach with girls. Such approaches can only increase and perpetuate gender differences in the classroom. Further, there was some suggestion that in a small number of cases teachers dealt more leniently with girls than with boys. There are no simple solutions to these issues, particularly because of the gendered nature of pupil behaviour in the classroom. However, awareness of the problems can help teachers to ensure that their own practices, at least, are not inequitable. Therefore, teachers may find it useful to reflect on their disciplinary practices, considering how often they tell off boys and girls, and whether the proportions actually reflect pupil behaviour. Further, they might attempt to note, or persuade a colleague to attend class and note for them, how much time is spent interacting with girls and boys in the classroom.

The second area is the misogyny and homophobia evident in the secondary school. This is a result of the hegemonic construction of compulsory heterosexuality in schools. As Holland et al. (1998) have observed, heterosexual relations and values are male dominated, locating power and agency in the male rather than the female, and denigrating the non-masculine (e.g. females and gay males). It seems important, then, that teachers are aware of this issue and try to stamp out homophobic or misogynist practices in the classroom. Girls and gay male pupils are particularly at risk as a result of these dominant constructions of heterosexuality, as demonstrated by the high incidence of sexual violence reported by the young female respondents in the book by Holland (1998) and the tragically high number of suicides among young gay men. Yet the research by Holland et al. is also useful for showing the immense pressure and limitation that these constructions of heterosexuality place on young men. Disruption of the gender cultures and the discourses perpetuating them seems important, although ways in which this could be done are far less clear. Possible strategies are discussed later in this book. However, concerning the use of sexist language, the suggestions offered by Salisbury and Jackson (1996) may be useful. They argue that teachers should ensure that they set a good example to pupils, checking that sex-biased terminology is not used in the language of the institution, in the way in which teachers address pupils or in the classroom materials. It also seems important that teachers take the issue of homophobic and sexist abuse seriously, disciplining pupils who practise such abuse and explaining why they are being disciplined.

4 Young People's Constructions of Gender and Status

Where the last chapter focused on devices used by pupils to construct their gender identities, this chapter focuses on pupils' oppositional constructions of gender and social status. During my previous work in the primary school I found that children often constructed masculinity and femininity as oppositional. Femininity was constructed as sensible and selfless, and masculinity as silly and selfish (these terms were invented by me, although the children themselves often used the words 'sensible' and 'silly' to describe the behaviour of girls and boys respectively).[1] These constructions had an impact on gendered power relations among primary school children. Girls appeared to believe that their sensible, facilitatory behaviour would win them favour from the teachers and other pupils. However, in fact the boys, in their oppositional roles as mischievous and self-centred, often took advantage of the girls' behaviour and used their advantage to dominate girls and other boys. By carrying out work in the secondary school, I was interested to see whether there was continuity or change in these sensible–selfless/silly–selfish positions. This issue is examined in the first section of this chapter. The second half of this chapter examines the gendered ways in which pupils resisted the teacher and the school agenda. The chapter aims to show the complexities of gender constructions in the classroom, as well as the impact of pupils' gender constructions on their social status and power position in school.

Sensible/Silly Constructions

In their discussions of gendered classroom behaviour, secondary school pupils reconceptualized the sensible/silly dichotomy in terms of maturity and immaturity. The notion of maturity was one I had noticed contributing to the construction of feminine sensibleness in the primary school classroom. Many secondary school girls talked of boys as being immature; for example, Gemma (Anglo, year 11) argues that boys "don't grow up as quick as girls

(.) an' some of 'em should still be in year *8* cos they, start *cussing girls* an' that, and hardly any of 'em get on with their work". In relation to the issue of gender and learning, many girls and some boys argued that girls mature faster than boys and therefore take learning more seriously or 'show off' less than boys (see Chapter 7). The work of Pattman et al. (1998b) supports these findings, showing that secondary school girls were vocal in their criticism of boys' classroom behaviour, branding it 'immature'. Pattman et al. found that although boys seemed to acquiesce with this view of themselves in the mixed-gender groups, in their single-sex groups they discussed girls' presentation of boys as immature with resentment, repositioning themselves as 'having a laugh' and girls as boring. By trivializing what they saw as superficial female pastimes and preoccupations, the boys also maintained that it is actually *girls*, rather than boys, who are immature.

Certainly, the boys did tend to actively 'mess about' in class more than did girls. It was common to see them stealing one another's bags and possessions (and fighting to reclaim them), throwing balls of paper and other things at one another, playing catch or football with balls of paper, rubbers and the like, and loudly abusing and making fun of one another. Such behaviour illustrates the 'silly', 'immature' or 'having a laugh' construction of masculinity. Girls had other ways of resisting the school regime as I discuss later in this chapter; however, their methods were not so overt, and they tended to chat quietly to their table-mates rather than shouting and running about the class as many boys did.

There were many examples of girls taking on quasi-teacher, sensible positions in opposition to the boys' 'silliness' in the classroom. Both Belotti (1975) and Walkerdine (1990) have noted the ways in which many girls position themselves like the teacher in the primary school; indeed, Walkerdine argues it is one of the few positions available to girls. As I found in the primary school, much of this oppositional gendered interaction appeared ritualized (Thorne, 1993). In the same way that female disapproval of boys' overt sexuality helped to construct boys as actively sexual and girls as shunning such overt sexuality, girls' disapproval of boys' 'silly' behaviour again serves to highlight the apparent difference between the sexes. An example of girls' 'sensible' disapproval of boys' 'silliness' is the high number of occasions when I observed girls telling rowdy boys to be quiet, sometimes explaining that they are trying to get on with their work. However, these 'sensible' quasi-teacher constructions were not unitary, as the following example demonstrates:

Notebook (21/10/98)
As I come into Ms K's year 8 registration class, Ms K is not there. A huge girl is blocking the doorway, and chatting to a friend. As a boy at

the other end of the corridor sticks his head out of a room into the corridor she yells, "Get back *in* there Tyrone, for registration". A boy from her class tries to leave, and she threatens him with her fist and literally chases him back into the class.

Hence this girl threatened a boy with physical punishment if he did not behave (punishment that she appeared quite capable of administering): a construction dramatically at odds with traditional femininity. Yet like the girls who told boys to be quiet, she was still constructing herself as the sensible/mature, pro-school, disapproving judge of boys' silly/immature behaviour. This quasi-teacher or teacher-helper construction could also be seen from the number of times girls offered to hand out sheets and books in class (and also in the teachers' constructions of girls, as I counted more occasions when they asked girls to hand things out than boys).

Contradictions and Complexities in Silly/Sensible Gender Constructions

There were also more overt contradictions to these dominant constructions of male silliness and female sensibleness. For example, many boys worked collaboratively in class, sometimes spending a lot of time helping and explaining work problems to other boys and girls. Conversely, some girls appeared to find it difficult to maintain the sensible construction. In a middle maths class at St Mark's School, Eve, a vocal Afro-Caribbean girl, took the role of quasi-teacher frequently, helping Aron, an Anglo-Irish boy sitting behind her, with his work (sometimes apparently against his will). In doing this she assumed a very patient, maternal manner. At one point after helping Aron, Eve then explained a point to a girl sitting in front of her. Ms Y asked Eve to go up and explain the calculations on the board for the benefit of the class:

John: G'wan Eve
Ms B: Now listen to Eve please {Eve goes back to her desk to get some different coloured pens and begins writing on the board}

Her selection of different colour pens for the task showed Eve's confident enthusiasm for the assignment. She explained to the class the calculations she had made, with some clarification from Ms Y. However, as she went on Eve began to find the calculations more difficult to explain. She struggled to find a way in which to make the class understand her point:

Eve:	Who does science here? {class groans and Eve laughs} *Listen* (.) {shouts} Listen, *listen* {she continues trying to explain the sum. Some pupils are muttering}
Ms B:	It's difficult to explain, she's doing very well
Eve:	{to the class} It's difficult to explain, cos I'm only 15 {the class laughs}
	Aron asks a question about Eve's sum on the board
Eve:	Are you *blind?*
Ms B:	There's no need to be sarcastic
Aron:	Yeah I only asked a question, no need to be *rude*

Eve attempted to assert her authority in her position of teacher but had little success in silencing the class, who continued to position her as a pupil. So she then adopted a strategy of repositioning herself as a pupil novice ("I'm only 15") to win the support of the class. In her position of pupil, Eve was also able to revert to non-sensible retorts to her classmates ("are you blind?"). Yet interestingly this occasioned a gender role reversal, as Aron's prim response seems to illustrate a sensible position and positions Eve as being silly and unreasonable.

A further partial reversal of the usual gender constructions in the classroom was evidenced in incidents where boys took on the quasi-teacher role. This happened on a number of occasions in one class at Sandyfields School, in which the teacher was unable to exert much discipline over the class. In this class, Saul and Wesley (both Afro-Caribbean) were two of the largest boys. They were consequently seen as 'hard'; but unlike many of the more stereotypically 'laddish' boys, Saul and Wesley also made it clear that they were keen to learn, and they participated attentively in the teacher's question and answer sessions. Yet the noise and disruption in the classroom, largely caused by other boys (there were more boys than girls in the class), often made listening to the teacher impossible. On some of the occasions where Ms P attempted to gain quiet, Saul and Wesley stepped in to help:

	Ms P tries to get the boys at the back to be quiet.
Ms P:	{shouting to boys at the back} If you want me to stop now, I will (.) but I'll give you something to do later (.) so you *listen* to me
Boy:	{laughing} All right then {hubbub continues}
Saul:	Hey you guys, shut up {silence falls}
	(Observer comment: it seems to be Saul's authority – rather than Ms P's remonstration – that is effective)
	Ms P begins talking about diameter, and boys at back begin talking and laughing again.
Saul:	Oi you lot, *Oi* {again, silence falls, and Ms P continues}

> *General hubbub continues while teacher tries to talk, then to*
> *quieten the class*

Girl: {to boys at the back} Shut up (.)

Wesley: {to boys at back} Can you just be *quiet*, man? {Silence falls}

These boys had strength and, consequently, authority, inscribed in their physiques. Wesley confirms this interpretation in his interview:

I: I mean, I've noticed *you* and one or two other boys actually *tell*ing some of the more rowdy boys to, shut up and be quiet, [how, how do you see that?

W: [Yeh (.) Well, well erm, they don't, they don't encourage other students to learn hard, they rather, erm, kind of dis*tract* them, to join them in, you know, making noise–

I: Mm

W: And I mean, that's wrong (.) so, I just shut them up, to listen to what the teacher's saying {grins}

I: {laughs} (.) How come the teacher can't do that do you think?

W: Well, erm, I think the teacher's fed up of you know shouting, you know, seem that, every day, we get this maths lessons, but they don't mind *her*, so, {laughs} I have to help her out

I: Do you think they take more notice of you?

W: (.) Um, first thing I would say is that, um, I think I'm, I think I'm quite um (.) {laughs} well, *tougher than them*, yeah, {I and W laugh – W continues laughingly} so I think they will listen to me

I: So you think that they're more scared of you [than they are the teacher, basically?

W: [Yeah, yeah {I and W laugh}

As such, Wesley and Saul's constructions of masculinity were secure despite their enthusiasm for learning or their 'sensible' siding with the teacher. Indeed, their ability to discipline other boys because of their physical superiority (i.e. the unspoken possibility of physical punishment that could be meted out if necessary) appeared to *enhance* their construction of masculinity. The female teacher seemed to be a foil in this construction, because she appeared contrastingly powerless in her lack of embodiment of such potential physical discipline.

Silliness and Humour

The finding by Pattman et al. (1998b) that boys in single-sex groups repositioned their supposed immaturity as 'having a laugh' seems significant when related to classroom behaviour. Almost all the classes had one, or a number of, 'class clowns'. There were variations among these pupils in terms of the cleverness of their humour, and the extent to which they were appreciated by the rest of the class. One or two appeared relatively unpopular and attempted to amuse the class or draw attention to themselves with little appreciation from their fellows. But more successful clowns were often among the most popular pupils in the class. As Luke (Anglo) explains in his interview, class clowns *could* be girls, but were more often boys. In no classes was there a single female 'clown' and no male, whereas the reverse was often true. Moreover, I noticed that many of the male class clowns appeared to be more easily accommodated or tolerated by the teacher: banter from boys seemed to be accepted more readily. Perhaps a boisterous, jovial, bantering style is less open to girls. Clarricoates (1980), Walkerdine (1990), Connolly (1998) and others have shown how girls' assertive or disruptive behaviour tends to be interpreted by teachers as more negative than does such behaviour in boys. Certainly if a girl adopted such a 'bantering' style with a male teacher it would be constructed as flirtatious, possibly positioning the girl concerned as sexually knowing and capricious. Being a class clown is at odds with the usual behaviour of girls in class, where the majority of girls do not usually actively call attention to themselves but rather chat and joke with other girls out of the teachers' hearing. Moreover, the construction of class clown is in direct opposition to the construction of femininity as sensible/mature.

For boys, on the other hand, the construction of class clown involves the opposite construction of silliness/immaturity, or 'having a laugh' as the boys put it. Thus such a role can play a useful and appropriate role in a boy's construction of himself as masculine. Social status is derived from amusing the class and from being seen to cleverly or bravely resist the teacher. This resistance has been shown by Skelton (1999) to be integral to many boys' construction of masculinity. Hence masculinity is constructed both through being 'silly' and through resisting the teacher. These dual factors are illustrated in the following examples:

Ms X: I'm gonna ask you again, any questions about the first section ?
Jacob: I 'ave a question Miss, why do we 'ave to do it? {friends titter}.

Ms D says she wants to check their homework
Vincent: What homework? You didn't set any homework
Ms W: Yes I did
Vincent: No you didn't
Ms W: Oh yes I *did*
Darren: {stylized} Oh no you didn't

Tonio:	Miss, does it 'ave to be four letters?
Ms J:	Ah, good question, very good question
Daniel:	{mock sincere} I was just gonna ask that {his table laughs}

Ms R asks the class if they use any dialect words

Ron:	Phwooaaar
Ms R:	{dubious} Mmm, what does that mean?
Ron:	Well, um, phwooaar, like you see a woman and say phwooaar

Ms R says that's onomatopoeia, and asks for other suggestions

Ron:	Bamberclot² {boys near him laugh}

Significantly, on many occasions I found myself laughing with the class at the boys' antics, which were often both clever and daring. One such occasion was when Mr Ledoux had to stand in for an absent teacher in an English class I was observing. Mr Ledoux had a strong accent, which Ron and Paul began imitating as soon as he appeared in the room. At one point the teacher approached their table:

Ron:	{speaking in Mr L's accent} *Mr Ledoux* {Mr Ledoux goes up to him warningly}
Ron:	{to Mr L, again in his accent, and leaning away from him} Keep your hands off me (.) Mr Ledoux dustbin man, get your hands off me {the others laugh}
Mr L:	[...] You *can't*.
Paul:	{Gasps} You *swore*
Mr L:	No I didn't
Ron:	Yes, you said 'you cunt' {laughter on table}
Mr L:	I did not
Paul:	Yes [you did
Ron:	[Yes you did
	Mr L points out to Ron that Mr K is in the class next door, and he can send Ron in there
Ron:	Go on then, go ahead
Mr L:	Right–
Ron:	I was only joking, {mock fervent} I apologize Mr Ledoux, I apologize {laughter on the table. Ron's mocking apologies go on for a while, and Mr L leaves the table}.
Ron:	{loudly in Mr L's accent} *Mr Ledoux*

With Mr Ledoux's accent, 'can't' did indeed sound rather like 'cunt', and I had to stop myself from giggling at the boys' opportunism. Yet my surreptitious amusement raises a serious issue. It is this very sort of behaviour for which boys are being criticized by educationalists and government ministers, who argue that boys' 'laddish' classroom behaviour is impeding their learning (see Francis, 1999a). When conducting the observation in schools I became increasingly aware of the appreciation I was affording class clowns, and the implications of this appreciation. Wit, daring and resistance to those in positions of power are appealing, and I feel sure I am not the only researcher to have found such incidents amusing and exciting. For example, who can resist an inward chuckle at the boys in Skelton's (1999) study having succeeded in breaking into and stealing the local police force's 'burglar-proof' police car? One of the classic criticisms of Paul Willis's (1977) study, where he focused on the antics of a group of 'lads' at school, is that he (an academic 'ear'ole') appears to have experienced exhilaration in his association with these hyper-masculine young men, apparently relishing their behaviour as exciting and enjoyable (Walkerdine, 1990). Teachers themselves often accommodated the behaviour of male class clowns when their behaviour was not overly challenging or offensive. Teachers sometimes engaged in banter with them and sometimes laughed at their jokes and tricks along with the pupils. The following incident provides an example of a teacher participating in a pupil's humorous conceit. The class had been asked to present statements and to decide whether each statement is opinion or fact:

Mr Q: Let's have yours, Jason

Jason: Er, Mr Q is bald= (.) {class laugh loudly} and is sick in the head {class laugh again}

Mr Q: What's the second bit?

Jason: That he's sick

Mr Q: That he's sick?

Jason: Yeah

Mr Q: In the head? Right, we've got two bits there, Mr Q is bald and sick in the head (.) {Rick indicates he wants to speak} would you split that statement into [two?

Rick: [Yeah, I was *about* to

Mr Q: Pardon?

Rick: I was *about* to

Mr Q: Sorry

Rick: It's a fact that you're bald, {laughter among pupils} cos you can see, like the *shine* on it {class laugh}, but it's an *opinion* that you're sick in the head {Mr Q nods that that's right}.

Mr Q was not offended by the boys' comments, indeed he appeared to actively encourage such banter. This is of course part of *his* construction of masculinity (Skelton, 2000). His ethos appeared to be that he can 'take it on the chin', and that the pupils should be able to do so too. As I pointed out in the previous chapter, this 'macho' style seemed more geared towards boys than girls.

Selfless/Selfish Constructions

In my study of gender constructions in primary schools, the use of role playing allowed me to watch who chose powerful roles, and who got first choice of roles, in mixed sex groups. I found that a construction of masculinity as assertive and demanding (selfish) constructed in opposition to a construction of femininity as facilitating (selfless) allowed boys to dominate the choice of role play scenario and to grab the most popular roles. However, it was the nature of my methodology that allowed me to observe this selfless/selfish gender construction so clearly. During my observation in secondary schools, there were fewer occasions in which such constructions could be examined. Although the boys' general domination of the classroom in terms of noise and use of physical space could be seen as 'selfish', there were few examples of girls directly constructing themselves as selfless in opposition. It is possible that their construction of femininity as 'selfless' had changed since primary school, but I lacked the opportunity to test this. It was my impression that generally girls simply tended to take a back seat in the classroom, allowing boys to dominate space and teacher time while they chatted together relatively quietly.

Yet what I had termed the 'selfish' construction of masculinity still appeared to be in evidence among secondary school boys. The following extracts from my observation notes provides examples:

2.00 p.m.
Ms P: Get ready for the lesson, then I'll give you (.) it shouldn't take
           that long {She switches the lights on. It makes a difference in
           the gloomy classroom. Clive gets up and goes to the light switch}
Clive: It hurts my eyes, Miss {he switches the lights off. Ms P says
           nothing} {Clive leaves the classroom. Ms P calls 'Clive' after
           him, to no avail}.

*2.00 p.m.   Matthew arrives in the class, finds a chair and sits. He takes an
           extra chair from David's table, which means that David's table
           is one short – David seems to simply accept this and goes to get
           another one for their table.*

I interpret this latter behaviour as another example of the masculinity hierarchy being delineated in interaction. The larger, more popular Matthew asserts his greater masculine status by taking the chair without asking, the unspoken implication being, 'I want this chair, and I know you won't dare challenge me'. David, used to such behaviour and resigned to it, amiably goes to find another chair. This also highlights how such constructions were not open to all boys all of the time.

In general, many boys were often assertive and inconsiderate of the feelings of others in the classroom, whether it be abusing one another or shouting out answers and comments, often over other pupils who were trying to speak. This 'selfish' construction overlapped with the dominant construction of masculinity as competitive: some boys took great delight in ridiculing or shouting down the answers of other boys and girls. This seemed to occur particularly in maths classes, perhaps because it is a more traditionally masculine subject than is English, but probably also because of the question and answer format which formed a sizeable part of the majority of maths lessons. In her interview, Leticia (mixed race, year 10) discussed how it is more often boys that respond to the teachers' questions in her maths class. I went on to ask,

I: Why do you think the girls aren't, aren't being so vocal? (.) I mean yourself excluded, cos as you say, in English you do make contributions

L: Cos, I don't know, I think that like, cos the boys are like, really (.) they tease, sort of like, tease girls a lot, but they only mess around they don't mean nothing by it, or nothing (.) but like, the girls take it, sort of to heart?

I: And, [and=

L: [And get it wrong

I: Boys do tease girls about it do they?

L: Yeah

I: They, so give me an example?

L: They go Uhn-nnn, dunce (.) like that

I: Right (.) do they do it to one another, if they get it wrong?

L: Ye:ah

I: So then why do you think girls are more sensitive about that?

L: I don't know, really (.) I just think they're, cos, (.) they're the boys, and (.)

I: Well, explain, explain, 'they're the boys'

L: Well cos like, me and my friends, we don't care cos like, we all, cuss the boys back and like we like (.) say our bit, but the other girls like Sara Jameson and all those quiet girls go "kay, shame"

I: Okay, yeah

L: And the boys, like, the girls feel the shame more than the boys do, the boys just don't care

Hence Leticia argues that some girls do not risk contributing in class for fear of being ridiculed and 'shamed' by boys. I observed such practices on many occasions during maths classes, although this competition and derision was usually expressed among boys. An example is provided by Philip's joy that Mr L discovers that Joel is behind Philip on a maths task:

	Mr L Asks Joel to answer question 10
Philip:	{gleeful} Oh good
Mr L:	Philip!
Joel:	Sir, I didn't get that far
Philip:	{gleeful} Why didn't you get that far?
Mr L:	Philip, I'll ask the questions
	Another boy struggles with the answer, and Philip volunteers to explain the answer. Mr L asks if he's able
Philip:	Yeah, I got it down to a fine art

In one maths class there was a long-standing competition between Denzel (Afro-Caribbean, year 10) and Wayne (Anglo, year 10), who were constantly trying to get ahead of one another or get more answers right. These boys sat on different sides of the classroom and kept a loud running commentary to one another across the class, in which one or two other boys were occasionally involved. However, on one occasion Denzel and Wayne, both apparently ahead with the task, were united in their competitive disdain for the rest of the class:

Wayne:	Too easy
	Ms W says she'll repeat the question – Denzel tells her not to, supported by Wayne
Denzel:	Oh don't Miss, if they ain't done it they ain't done it
	Ms W reads out the question again
Wayne:	Aw this is embarrassing

Such academic competitiveness raises the issue of masculinity and learning. Some researchers have argued that to be seen to work hard and to take an interest in schoolwork is at odds with dominant constructions of masculinity (Salisbury and Jackson, 1996; Younger and Warrington, 1996; Pickering, 1997). However, Mac an Ghaill (1994) and others have pointed out that there are different ways of 'doing' masculinity, academic competition being one of them. This may particularly be the case in traditionally masculine subjects such as maths. Moreover, the boys' boasting often implied the notion of 'effortless achievement', which Bourdieu and Passeron (1979) have argued is the mark of what is seen to be a 'true' (i.e. middle-class, white, male) academic.

Gender Constructions and Power

The construction of silliness/'having a laugh' and selfishness taken up by some boys often endowed them with power in the classroom. This power was derived both from the prestige that such constructions earned and from the ability to use these constructions to put down or threaten other pupils (and teachers). There was also evidence that *boys'* perceptions of acceptable behaviour in girls impacted on girls' behaviour. Holland et al. (1998) argue that the 'male in the head' (their metaphor for the masculine surveillance in a male-dominated society) regulates the behaviour of both boys and girls, and ensures that girls conform to what men see as desirable female behaviour. An example can be provided by interaction between Joan and Matthew in a year 10 English class. Joan (mixed race) is a vocal girl, almost of the class clown mode, who relishes attention. Matthew is the popular Afro-Caribbean boy who was reported above taking a chair from Daniel's table. The class has been acting out a court scene, in which Joan is a barrister:

9.48 a.m.	*Joan begins summing up, seriously. After a while she becomes self-conscious and falters a little*
Joan:	…he, um, oh (.) he became a very difficult man…
Matthew:	{quietly and sarcastically to Joan) *Rabbit rabbit*
Joan:	{to Matthew} Yeah well, but no-one else is talking, innit? (.) um= {she falters and trails off}

Matthew and another boy then took over the summing up. It seemed that even a usually vocal and assertive girl like Joan could not continue in the face of sarcastic disapproval from one of the most popular boys in the class.

As in the primary school, the girls' constructions of sensible/mature femininity appeared to earn the appreciation of other girls, and occasional approval from the teacher, and hence could be seen as potentially powerful. Yet in terms of the general classroom interaction, girls' sensibleness/maturity meant taking a back seat while the classroom interaction and teacher attention was dominated by the boys. In this sense it is arguable that, as in the primary school, the girls' constructions of femininity actually meant abdicating power to the (silly/having a laugh/selfish) boys. However, it is also possible that such gender constructions have different implications for *learning* than they do for classroom domination. This issue will be explored further in Chapter 7.

Resistance

The discussion of the antics of male class clowns has already illustrated how these and other boys drew on 'silly' constructions of masculinity to resist the teacher and school ethos. However, despite the common construction of sensible maturity favoured by some girls, few girls were simply passive in the classroom, and many were involved in actively resisting the teacher or school generally. This is not a new finding: Riddell (1989), Anyon (1983) and Lees (1993) have all shown in detail how girls resist the school system in various ways. These studies also show, however, how girls tend to express resistance in different ways to boys. I have already discussed how girls tended to chat and laugh together, often at the back of the class, but how such behaviour was less noticeable or problematic to the teacher than were the boys' louder interruptions. I found that one of the most frequent forms of overt classroom resistance among girls (rather than simply chatting to friends, for example) took the form of expressions of boredom or tedium. Crucially, this expression was usually not verbalized but signalled in various silent ways. For example, I noticed one girl wearing headphones and listening to her personal stereo in class, and a number of girls apparently asleep in class (some on a number of different occasions). I did not observe any boys asleep or feigning sleep during my observation. Pretending to be asleep could of course be interpreted as 'silly' behaviour, yet I would argue that it is rather intended to suggest a languid disdain for the business of school: in this way such resistance does not necessarily disrupt the girls' construction of themselves as being mature, as it suggests an aloof disinterest in classroom process.

Some girls did engage a silly/'having a laugh' construction in order to noisily resist the teacher. An example can be seen when Samantha and Maisie (both Anglo) were communicating across the class and Ms D became angry and sent them out into the corridor. The girls in the corridor could then be heard from the classroom shouting and laughing, to the amusement of many in the class and to the annoyance of Ms D. After going out to remonstrate with them twice, Ms D brought Samantha and Maisie back into the room, apparently because of the disruption they were causing outside. Hence although loud, bantering or confrontational resistance was more often practised by boys, these and other girls were vocal in the classroom and were as likely as boys to 'cheek' the teacher, reminding us that such behaviour is not exclusive to boys.

There were other forms of resistance used by both boys and girls. Sometimes all the pupils joined in together; for example, in response to Ms X's instruction to put their pens down and listen, boys and girls alike whacked their pens down on the desks, making a clattering noise. Another method of resistance was an appeal to rationality in confrontation with the teacher, or endeavouring to actually patronise or belittle the teacher. This form of resistance was drawn upon by some girls but was used far more frequently by boys. And on each occasion in which I identified its use during my observation, it was used against female teachers. The two instances I recorded of girls taking this approach are set out below:

Ms X: {to Shazna on the back table} *Shazna I told you to move*
Shazna: *How?* (.) It's even more crowded over here, Miss
             {*a girl at the back is whispering*}
Ms X: You work on your own please.
Girl: {quietly} Yep (.) We *are.*

In these examples the girls draw on discourses of rationality to position themselves as innocent and the teacher as unreasonable. The following exchange between Ms P and Clive echoes these processes, although Clive is distinctly more confrontational than were the girls:

Ms P: Clive (.) *Clive*
Clive: I'm not *talk*ing, Miss (.) why do you always call *my* name? I
             ain't even talking y'know
Ms P: In this class there are thirty of them, why did I say 'Clive'?
Clive: You tell *me*

These examples show the pupils drawing on discourses of rationality to disrupt the traditional relationship between pupil and teacher, positioning the teacher as unreasonable. In the following examples pupils go even further; they reverse the traditional pupil/teacher dichotomy and construct the pupils (male) as bearing authority and the teacher (female) as being child-like and answerable to them:

             Ms X tells the class to hand in their papers
Ms X: And if you can't hear me you should wash out your ears
Victor: Miss, you're tryin'a get lippy with us, ain't ya? {a couple of
             pupils laugh, as they all hand papers to the front and begin to
             exit the room}.

             *A balled-up paper falls near one of the girls' tables as Ms P is
             addressing the class*
Ms P: {shouts} Who threw this paper just now? (.) I want you to be
             honest with yourself, pick it up and put it in the bin (.) {she
             suggests that a girl sitting near it threw it, but the girl says it hit
             her back, and argues it couldn't have been her because it landed
             behind her back}

Marcus:	Miss here's my paper {he shows her his paper to show it can't have been him that threw the paper} (.) I'm gonna pick this one up and put it in the bin {he speaks slowly, even patronisingly, and picks up the ball of paper, approaching the bin with it}.
Ms P:	{shouting at Marcus} What, I don't want you to pick it up, the person who has thrown it will pick it up {to class} Don't be coward
Marcus:	{laughing, Indian accent} Don't be coward
Ms P:	The person who has thrown it can pick it up as well
Marcus:	Look, Miss {again, he speaks slowly and patronizingly, and moves to put the paper ball in the bin} (.) that would just resolve your trouble
Ms K:	{giving up} (.) That's not very nice whoever has done it
Clive:	{ironic} That's what I was thinking

Wesley:	{severe} Miss, we need that paper, please
	(Observer comment – certain boys in this class seem to subtly undermine Ms P by being more 'teacher-like' than she is)
	Ms P continues discussing the maths problem. Wesley guesses the answer and mumbles it while Ms P continues. When she announces the answer (apparently the same as Wesley's), the latter is indignant
Wesley:	Miss, what did I say?
	Ms K continues and repeats the answer
Wesley:	Duhhh, I *said* that

Of course, the majority of these examples all involve the same teacher, whom I have already noted as having a discipline problem with her class. Yet the fact that I did not observe these methods of resistance being practised on male teachers seems potentially salient and may be an interesting area of further research. The use of discourses about rationality and notions of individual freedom, which are highly valued in the West, enable pupils to undermine the teachers' authority and construct themselves as powerful by positioning themselves as more rational that the teacher.

To conclude this section, I have shown that although it was more often boys who loudly, aggressively or humorously resisted the teacher these strategies were drawn on by some girls too. Girls' methods of resistance were generally quieter than those of boys; for example, chatting and laughing together, or dramatically feigning boredom. Not all boys used vocal methods of resistance either: some groups of boys also chatted and laughed together quietly. Yet in terms of status, vocal, aggressive or humorous resistance, particularly on the part of boys, did appear to bring individual pupils kudos among their fellows.

Discussion

In terms of continuity or change in dominant constructions of gender between primary and secondary school, it seemed that the oppositional construction of 'sensible' femininity contrasted with 'silly' masculinity remained intact, although these positions had been reconfigured as 'maturity' and 'immaturity' (or 'having a laugh') in pupils' talk. There was less evidence of a construction of feminine selflessness, although this may in part have been due to my changed research methods. However, constructions of masculine selfishness remained evident, particularly overlapping with a competitive and overbearing construction of masculinity adopted by a number of boys.

As in the primary school, these gendered positions were by no means fixed or adopted by all pupils, with considerable diversity and overlaps in constructions on the parts of both girls and boys. However, it did still seem to be the case that a dominant construction of boys as irresponsible and competitive allowed many boys to dominate the classroom space and interaction, and to exercise power over girls and other boys. Moreover, using the construction of 'silly' masculinity in the sense of 'having a laugh' in the classroom enabled individual boys to express their 'proper' masculinity and to gain status both by being seen as 'properly masculine' and by entertaining the class. Whitehead (1998) suggests that less able boys resort to laddish behaviour to construct their masculinity. I found boys in middle *and* top sets just as likely to play the class clown and to humorously resist the teacher. However, there was some limited evidence from my study that boys in top set classes were somewhat less likely to take directly and aggressively confrontational stances with the teachers.

I have shown how the former kind of masculine, 'having a laugh' behaviour was often tolerated or even encouraged by teachers – and indeed I recognized that I often found it appealing. Hence adults could also contribute to the increased status with which boys engaging in such behaviour were rewarded by their peers. This finding is significant and should give pause for thought: it is precisely this kind of disruptive, silly/'having a laugh' behaviour that some commentators have blamed for boys' underachievement. If this is the case then the collusion with, or acceptance of, such behaviour on the part of teachers and educationalists may be implicated in the perpetuation of boys' comparative underachievement. This issue will be explored further in later chapters.

5   Young People's Talk about Gender and Studentship

So far, we have seen how oppositional constructions of gender are perpetuated in the classroom and the various sorts of gendered behaviour that such constructions entail. We have also seen how important the maintenance of these gender constructions can be for young people's social status (while recognizing that there is also much diversity in the behaviour of young people). But what impact do these gender constructions have on the young people's perceptions of learning and ability? This chapter examines the young people's opinions on gender and learning, drawn from the interview data. It discusses their perceptions of 'the ideal pupil', and goes on to show how such notions, including perceptions of ability, have shifted in terms of gender.

The Ideal Pupil

Young people were asked to describe the ideal pupil. Attributes listed were extremely diverse: thirty-seven different characteristics were mentioned (see Appendix 3), from 'hard-working' to 'good-looking'. Most pupils listed more than one attribute. It soon became clear that my question about the ideal pupil should have specified a perspective (e.g. 'from a teacher's point of view' or 'from a pupil's point of view'), because some pupils described their own ideal, whereas others described what Sara (Anglo, year 10) refers to as "an all-round goody-goody". However, the latter pupils were a small minority: most pupils described what they perceived to be the consensus view of a good pupil. Indeed, many were at pains to point out that the ideal pupil should have good social skills and have fun (though possibly outside lessons), as well as being hard-working. For example, Athena (mixed race, year 11) explains of the ideal pupil, "Um I think of someone that, who has their fun outside school but when they come into school they just do their work and then, but they still have a social life afterwards, cos some people, they just do their work an' thass all they *do* (.) {laughs}". Ron (mixed race, year 10) identifies *himself* as the personification of the ideal pupil, but does so in terms of his classroom persona rather than learning style:

I: Right, well describe your learning style and what makes it so ideal

R: Er, *funny* (.) come in casual, don't always dress like the way the teacher say, er (.) *collar* up, cos that's like the way, er, not everyone does it, {I laugh} er (.) good hairstyle {I laugh} {R hastily}, *not today, not today*, (.) cos I didn't put enough mousse in it {I laugh} (.) er, just, thass' it innit, like, just, er, stay out of trouble, don't cause any trouble and when people get into trouble you can just laugh at them an' that.

That the ideal pupil is *not* a swot or 'goody-goody' was specified by five pupils, and nineteen others argued that the ideal pupil is fun, or charismatic, with an active social life. Felicity (Afro-Caribbean, year 11) maintains that the ideal pupil is sporty and good-looking, explaining the dangers of being identified as a swot: "If you're not, up there and, popular, you seem to get bullied". Hence regarding the issue of the ideal pupil, the distinction between being what Denzel (Afro-Caribbean, year 10) refers to as a "*nerd*y type" and a "*smarty* type" appeared very important to many pupils, suggesting a thin line between being a good pupil and a 'nerd', which carried heavy penalties if unwittingly transgressed. This delineation seemed to be important for girls as well as boys.

Because the attributes that pupils listed the ideal pupil as possessing were so diverse, often only one or two pupils listed a particular attribute, and consequently it initially appeared that there was little generalizable difference in pupils' opinions on the issue according to gender. Only a few points stood out; for example, that three boys said specifically that the ideal pupil is 'like me', whereas no girls displayed such confidence. Three boys said the ideal pupil must have charisma, and three more said good looks, where only one girl argued each point. However, most of the subtle differences in opinion between genders concerned *behaviour*. As I progressed with the analysis I noticed that more boys appeared concerned with the ideal pupils' exemplary behaviour than did girls. So, for instance, more boys than girls remarked that the ideal pupil would be well-behaved, obey the teacher's instructions, get on well with or respect the teacher, be punctual and would not get into trouble. In turn, girls seemed more preoccupied with the ideal pupil's learning style: more girls than boys commented that the ideal pupil would be a hard worker, a good learner, serious about work and try hard. Sure enough, in counting all the pupils' comments I found that fifty-eight of the girls' comments and forty-eight of the boys' comments related to the ideal pupil's approach to learning. In turn, only twenty-two of the girls' comments and thirty-five of the boys' comments related to disciplinary behaviour. Almost equal numbers of girls' and boys' comments focused on the personal and personality attributes of the ideal pupil (e.g. a good social life, good looks, fun, charisma, not a swot, is a swot).

Regarding the apparent trend for boys to place a greater emphasis on behaviour and girls on approach to learning, I suggest that this reflects both classroom experience and dominant discourses relating to gender and achievement. In earlier chapters I explained how my classroom observation supported the findings of researchers such as Spender (1982), Younger and Warrington (1996), Howe (1997) and Younger et al. (1999), who describe boys as generally noisier and more boisterous in the classroom than girls. Boys consequently gain more of the teacher's attention, in terms of banter, help with work and approbation. Because it tends to be boys who are most frequently in trouble with the teacher, boys may come to see this as an issue that particularly stands out in terms of their studentship. This can only be encouraged by the currently prolific discourse on 'failing boys', which positions adolescent masculinity and its associated lack of discipline or respect for authority as 'a problem' (Griffin, 1998; Francis, 1999a). Boys are, of course, aware of this discourse and issues around it, which I shall discuss later in this chapter.

Male and Female Ability at Different Subjects

Sixty-six per cent of girls (thirty-three) and 84 per cent of boys (forty-two) said that male and female pupils have the same ability at all subjects. Seventeen girls (34 per cent) and eight boys (16 per cent) argued that they do not have the same ability. Hence two-thirds of girls and well over three-quarters of boys maintained that subject ability is not gendered. This illustrates a change in perceptions since Femena's study (reported in Spender, 1982), where the majority of boys and many girls said that girls are no good at maths. It even marks a change since Whitehead's (1996) more recent research, which showed that pupils tended to believe girls and boys to be good at different things. Contemporary pupils are far more aware and supportive of issues of equal opportunity than has been the case in the past (Francis, 1998a; Volman and Ten Dam, 1998). Moreover, the increased success of girls at subjects like maths and science at GCSE level may have impacted on the young people's perceptions of ability. Certainly the pupils' preferences for different subjects have become more diverse than in the past. While still reflecting a traditionally gendered pattern to some extent (with girls particularly disliking 'science' subjects, and boys particularly disliking language subjects), a much larger number of girls included subjects such as maths and science among their favourites than has been the case in previous studies (Francis, 2000).

Indeed, nearly twice as many of the 25 per cent of pupils who argued that male and female pupils do *not* have the same ability in all subjects were *girls*: this hints at what I found in their responses. It was often not notions of *female* inferiority that were leading pupils to respond in this way, but a notion of *male* inferiority. Spender (1982) argued that teachers expected boys to be brighter than girls, and that this expectation was reflected in pupils' perceptions. However, two decades on, the situation appears to have altered considerably: female superiority at some or all subjects was the most frequently provided explanation among those pupils arguing that there are gender differences in subject ability. Seven girls and four boys provided such answers.

Six girls and two boys said that boys and girls tend to be better at different subjects. Of these eight pupils, six came from the same class, and one girl told me that her teacher had told this class that boys tend to be better at maths problems, and girls better at English and languages. This opinion certainly appeared to be reflected in the young people's responses, as four of the six pupils from this teacher's class claimed that boys tend to be better at maths, and girls better at English and languages. (The other two pupils from this class did not explain their reasoning for saying that boys and girls tend to be good at different subjects.) The responses of these pupils obviously denote a traditional view of the different abilities of the sexes, and one that has previously been reflected in levels of achievement at different subjects according to gender. However, as was observed in Chapter 1, although boys still lag behind girls in terms of achievement at languages, recently girls have caught up with boys in science and maths at GCSE level. The remaining three pupils who said boys and girls tend to be better at different subjects actually presented girls as being better at maths and/or science, and said that boys tend to be better at subjects like drama and PE.

Two girls and one boy gave examples of subjects that they thought boys excel at without mentioning girls (all three said PE, and one girl added technology). Three pupils did not provide explanations for their answers. Although five pupils (four girls and one boy) said that girls are better at all subjects, no pupils claimed that boys are better at all subjects.

Although comparatively few pupils argued that there are gender differences in subject ability, the responses of those that did suggest that knowledge of girls' success at GCSE level may have 'trickled down' to some pupils and is impacting on their conceptions of female ability. A discourse of female ability is now competing with a traditional discourse of gender differences in ability at different subjects, the latter of which was reflected in the reported statement of the class teacher and her pupils' responses to my interview question. A further aspect impacting on these responses might be the hegemony of equal opportunities discourse *as applied*

I: (.) Okay, so this is quite interesting for me, you're saying that, um, the *boys* get respect, by sort of, um, arguing with the teacher,[and being loud and rowdy in class=

F: [*Mm* (.) Mmm

I: =Whereas *girls*, can still get respect, even if they're quite studious, is it?

F: Yeah

Hence Felicity and others specifically support the arguments of researchers such as Salisbury and Jackson (1996), Pickering (1997) and Skelton (1997), who maintain that boys' constructions of masculinity do not fit well into the culture and ethos of school, and that indeed boys' successful construction of masculinity is often based on resistance to the school and teacher. Maisie (Anglo, year 10) describes the status boys derive from being disruptive, and the consequences for girls' and boys' learning:

I: Do you think that, um, being male or female makes a difference to being a good student?

M: (.) Erm, yeah, I *suppose it does in a way*, cos (.) when you're, um, sort of a *girl* and everything, like, a lot, I think (.) the teachers put a lot more responsibility on to you because they think you're more responsible than a lot of the boys

I: *Why* do they think that?

M: {sighing} Cos the boys are just, mess about all the time, I know, like, there's a difference between, the *girls*, the *girls* get on and do their work and they're not, *class nerds* or, anything, but, I think the boys if you get on with the work and, do it and, everythink like that you're sort of classed as a nerd, and if you don't do=

I: Why do you think that *is*?

M: It's just the way things *go* in the school, it's like *status* innit?, and then everyone that sort of don't get on with their work and messes about and don't do their homework and that, they're sort of the *popular* boys so, everyone knows that sort of them ones don't do no work, so the girls get the responsib–, er the teachers put the responsibility on the girls cos they don't, have that sort of *status*, so– (.)

I: And that pushes the girls harder then, presumably?

M: Yeah (.) yeah I suppose so

I: I'm wondering why you've got that difference, you know, where, to be an acceptable, popular girl you can still, work hard–

M: Yeah

I: But, for a boy you can't

M: I know, I don't *know* why that is, I just think, just like, cos *boys'*
     popularity is *different* to *girls* (.) boys' popularity is based on like,
     erm, how *hard* they are and what *sports* they take part in and everythink
     and sort of academic achievement don't really come *into* it, so–
I: Is it all right for them to be *thick*?
M: (.) Yeah, a lot of them *are* {I laugh} (.) {laughing} a *lot* of them *are*,
     I think *most* of boys in this school are (.) but, um, I don't *know* why, I
     think that's just the way it is

This female disapproval of boys' masculine culture was expressed by several
girls. Throughout our discussions of gender and learning, discourses of
female superiority and female maturity were expressed by many girls,
supporting the findings of Phoenix et al. (forthcoming), who found that
girls were very vocal in their criticism of the behaviour of boys. When
discussing the apparent peer pressure and distraction that boys experience
in relation to disruptive classroom behaviour, many girls positioned their
friendships as being different from those of boys. Girls were presented as
more accepting of work orientation and application. And although Felicity
maintains that girls still need to be pretty in order to be popular, other girls
and boys positioned girls as less judgmental and more supportive of one
another than are boys with their friends. Boys' friendships tended to be
presented as competitive and conditional. Shanice (Afro-Caribbean, year
10) explains, "with um relationships with girls, s'more, like, I dunno, they
talk about things more, and that? and they help each other, with *boys*, it's
not seen to do good at schoolwork, they do good if they're alone, but, if
their friends are not doing work, like, good things, then they don't, either".
Paul's (Anglo, year 10) comments express this view of boys' friendships as
pressured and competitive particularly clearly:

P: [.] sometimes, *boys* are like *scared* to go to a teacher to ask for help,
     cos it might, affect their, like, um, (2) *popularity* in the school (.) like
     some=
I: Street-cred, yeah
P: Yeah, someone would call, them, '*bod*' or whatever, and they wouldn't
     like it so they wouldn't *ask* for help anymore
I: Why is that, why are boys more concerned not to be called 'spoddy'
     or 'boddy', or whatever you call it, than, um, than girls?
P: (.) Um, dunno, it's like a *masculinity* thing I think, s'like, if, if you're
     a bod you're s, supposedly *weak*, and, if you're like, *bad*, and like,
     rude to teachers and that (.) you get more friends or somethink like
     that, but, I, in my personal opinion, I think, if you're *bad*, like, most

people go around with you cos they're scared of you, and, like, don't wanna get beaten up or whatever

Paul had argued that this affects boys' ability to be good pupils. When I asked Paul, then, why this peer pressure does not appear to affect girls so much, he presented girls as more practical and focused than boys. He went on to argue that some boys still take their basic educational achievement and future employment for granted due to sexist assumptions, summarizing, "[boys] think, 'oh I'm a boy, I'll probably get good marks, *anyway*'".

Finally, one boy (Mohammed, African, year 11) identified the discourse of boys' underachievement as impacting on gender and good studentship. He initially presented a similar view to many other pupils of boys being "more hyper" than girls and "more into *playing* than studying". However, when I asked him what he thinks causes these gender differences, he replies,

M: (2) S'just (.) probably (.) like cos like, just say you were watching telly, *television*, and they're always like saying, 'oh boys, like, females are better than boys' and that, and the boys probably just, just, *react* to that, and just behave like

I: Have you reacted to it, do you think?

M: Nah (.) nah, I, nah

I: But you think that the TV and, and the media give the impression that girls are doing better?

M: Yeah

I: Can you give me an, an example of that, or are you just talking generally?

M: Nah, I'm talking, I'm talking generally, but I've *seen* like, I've seen the media, like they, and the *teachers* as well, saying that *girls*, are more like (.) probably more successful

Thus Mohammed suggests that a self-fulfilling prophecy is occurring in relation to boys' educational achievement: boys hear that they are underachieving, and that girls are doing better, so they give up and behave as they believe they are expected to behave. Although I have no evidence to support Mohammed's view, it is interesting to note that in the early 1980s researchers such as Stanworth (1981) and Clarricoates (1980) demonstrated that teachers' low expectations of girls were undermining their confidence and causing a self-fulfilling prophecy. There is little reason to suppose that such expectations would not have the same effect on boys.

Mohammed blames teachers as well as the media for propagating the view that girls are better at learning. In their discussions of gender and learning, many girls and boys mentioned the impact of teachers and teacher expectations of boys and girls. Some supported Mohammed's argument that teachers have higher expectations of girls than of boys. For example, in response to my question whether being male or female makes a difference to being a good pupil, Athena (mixed race, year 11) replies,

A: (.) Nah, I think they get treated differently though at school
I: That's interesting, explain
A: Because, I think the teachers put more pressure on the *girls* than the boys, because they *expect* the boys to be, causing, the um (.) er detention and that they're always messing around and they *expect* it, because they never pay no *attention* (.) so all the pressure's put on the girls to do well

It is hard to separate the teachers' expectations here from what Athena reports to be boys' actual behaviour ("they never pay no attention"). In the talk of a number of pupils, discourses of female superiority (positioning boys as disruptive or inadequate) and equity (criticizing apparent gender discrimination by teachers) were used simultaneously, again demonstrating the extent to which contradiction can exist apparently without fracture in pupils' talk about gender (Francis, 1998a). An example is Shamin's (South Asian, year 10) response to my question about the 'good' pupil:

I: Um, do you think being male or female makes a difference to being a good student, or not being a good student?
S: No but, erm, *some* of the teachers *can* be sexist, I reckon (.) for instance I had this teacher who's like, she would *al*ways be sexist towards the boys, she would like she would wu–, say like, if they weren't doing anything she would like invent something to say they were making trouble and stuff (.) and the girls [did it
I: [Really? That's interesting
S: A lot of the teachers seem to prefer girls I think
I: Why do you think that might be?
S: Because, *they* do their work more, they're not as naughty as boys (.)
I: So being male or female *does* tend to make a difference?
S: Yeah, sometimes, and it, it's not, really the (.) the way the boys behave, that's what, puts the teachers off boys

Shamin begins by drawing on an equity discourse to criticize 'sexist' teachers who seem to prefer girls. Yet when I ask her why this might be, she draws on a discourse of female superiority to explain that girls are more work-oriented and less 'naughty' than boys, apparently justifying the teacher's negative perceptions of boys. Sabina (South Asian, year 10) is more explicit, reporting, "My maths teacher said that 'If I had a choice I just would teach girls' (.) and, boys *did* scream out 'sexist'", but arguing that her teacher's view is justified because the girls in her class are better behaved than the boys.

However, other pupils maintained that teachers simply discriminated according to gender in their general attitudes towards pupils. Raymond (African, year 10) maintains that teachers prefer females. He explains,

R: Yeah, like if I ask, if I'm answering a question (.) some teachers won't listen, even some other boys answer questions, the teacher won't listen, but if a girl answers it, exactly the same question, just copies us, she will say 'oh yeah that's right', an' all that

When I ask whether he thinks boys are discriminated against, he answers at length:

R: Yeah, because people are talking about how women are not getting equal rights and all that (.) they're getting, thass' the thing, I think that women now be getting equal rights when boys are now getting, are *not* getting equal rights, so it might as well, none of you, if none of you's gonna get equal rights, better shut up then and don't say shit

I: (.) Boys and girls?

R: *Yeah* (.) cos they're saying about how *girls*, are, people are discriminating girls, but what, they don't think about *boys* getting discriminated because they think that boys are all *macho* and all that, but not all boys are like that, some boys *do* want to learn=

I: Mm

R: But they just think that boys are all nuisances.

Raymond's resentment is clearly articulated, drawing heavily on the discourse of 'poor boys' identified by Epstein et al. (1998). His words also highlight the findings of Volman and Ten Dam (1998) that many secondary school pupils believe women now have equality with men. Yet importantly, his talk reflects the common assumption that such increased opportunity for females has been bought at the expense of males (Yates, 1997).

Rick (Afro-Caribbean, year 11) claims that teachers are "lenient towards girls". This perception was supported by a number of other pupils – often, but not exclusively, boys. Craig (Afro-Caribbean, year 11) explains, "Say if I was to do, something wrong, and the teacher would maybe, teacher's reaction would be *much*, you know, he'd be much, *quick*er, to take action, than if it was a female, that's what I think". Other researchers such as Wing (1997), Pickering (1997) Younger et al. (1999) and Phoenix et al. (forthcoming) have also articulated the feelings of many boys that they are disciplined more quickly and severely than are girls. Indeed, Pickering (1997) cites boys' resentment at teachers' apparently discriminatory disciplinary practices as a potential factor in boys' alienation from and underachievement at school. He does, however, note the difficulty in separating whether or not teachers are justified in disciplining boys more harshly than girls. It is the same difficulty expressed in some of the girls' apparently contradictory statements about teachers, boys and discipline discussed above. Does the fact that boys are disciplined more frequently than girls by teachers show that teachers are discriminating against boys, or that boys generally tend to be louder and more disruptive than girls? I have already discussed in Chapters 1 and 2 how the strategies of resistance of the boys tended to be louder and more challenging to the teacher than those of the girls, and consequently the boys gained more of the teachers' approbation.

This question of discipline also raises the issue of the attention teachers devote to boys: some researchers have argued that boys' greater vocality in the classroom, whether learning oriented or disruptive, draws the teacher's attention towards them and away from girls (e.g. Spender, 1982). Hence even if this extra teacher attention is disciplinary, girls are also penalized by gaining less attention from the teacher. This traditional feminist argument is explicitly supported by Donna (Afro-Caribbean, year 11):

I: Do you think being male or female makes a difference to that (.) the ideal [student?

D: [Yes

I: Explain *why*, I mean it comes back to what we were saying=

D: *Be*cause, they say that, it seems that the teachers always show more attention to the boys than to the girls (.) er, I know it's only one teacher and thirty pupils but even then sometimes they pay more attention to the boys than to the girls (.) and if a *boy* was to do something and a girl was to do something I, I get the *feeling* that it would be, it would be worse for the girl to do it, cos they expect more from the girl than they do from the boy

I: Wh, why is that?

D: Dunno, it, it just feels like that sometimes

I: And when you say that the boy gets more attention, say something about that

D: It, it's not even something *good* he'll be doing–

I: Yeh

D: Sometimes it'll be something bad, but it's just like they get more attention than the rest of the, class

I: (.) So like the boy takes up more of the teacher's=

D: Time

I: Time

Interestingly, she also notes a point made by Clarricoates (1980), Walkerdine (1990), Connolly (1998) and Reay (1999) that when a girl does behave overtly disruptively she tends to be punished and viewed more severely by the teacher than are boys, owing to the teacher's constructions of what is properly feminine. This argument obviously sits in opposition to the boys' claims that teachers are more lenient with girls than with boys. However, perhaps it might be the case that *usually* boys tend to be disciplined more frequently, whereas girls' quieter forms of resistance tend more often to be ignored; yet if a girl breaks these norms she will be penalized more heavily by the teacher than would boys in the same circumstances. Further research is needed to establish whether there is any evidence for any of these claims concerning gender and classroom discipline in school. It is an issue that warrants serious consideration, particularly bearing in mind the resentment expressed by a number of pupils in discussion of this issue, and the possible alienation from the classroom which might be experienced as a result.

Discussion

The main finding concerning the question of 'good' studentship and the question of gendered ability is the large number of pupils who argued against gender difference, maintaining that one's gender does not affect one's ability at different subjects or whether or not one is a good pupil. I have argued that this illustrates the strength of equity discourses among pupils. This should be seen as a positive finding for feminists and liberal educationalists generally, so long as it does not reflect an ignorance of continuing gender discrimination (as suggested by Volman and Ten Dam, 1998). However, in the responses of young people who argued that girls and boys are better at various subjects, and that gender *does* impact on good studentship, a significant majority maintained that girls are better pupils, and better at various subjects. This highlights a discursive change: boys are no longer seen as 'naturally' superior to girls, and their masculinity is being problematized. Moreover, it demonstrates a change in girls' constructions of femininity. Studies in the 1970s and 1980s found that secondary school girls believed that to be seen as clever would repel men, because intelligence was not seen as desirable in women (Maccoby and Jacklin, 1974; Spender, 1982). Hence girls sought to avoid being seen as clever, and sometimes 'acted the bimbo' for the benefit of men and boys (Spender, 1982). The findings in this chapter illustrate how this construction has shifted: many girls articulated a confidence in female educational abilities and often derided boys' apparent lack of academic application. Displays of academic application were seen to be more problematic for boys than for girls.

The young people's talk about gender difference regarding studentship reflected and highlighted the two different perspectives found in discourses about 'boys' underachievement'. These are the perspectives that explain the relative underperformance of boys as being the fault of teachers, feminists and educational policy (expressed via narratives of 'poor boys' and 'blaming women'; see Epstein et al., 1998), and an opposing perspective that problematizes male behaviour.

6 Young People's Views of the Importance of Gender and Education for their Lives

This chapter examines the young people's talk about gender issues outside school and about their educational and career aspirations. So, having discussed young people's constructions of gender in school during the last three chapters, this chapter explores the ways in which they constructed gender as an issue affecting their lives in the wider society, and also the ways in which gender appears to impact on their own aspirations. In asking them about this, I hoped that the pupils' views on gender in the wider society might provide me with information with which to reflect on their classroom behaviour and their approaches to school and learning. The second half of this chapter focuses on the perceptions of girls concerning their future work and life in the workplace: the findings are applied to the issue of the increasing educational success of girls.

Young People's Views of the Impact of Gender in the Wider Society

One of the interview questions pupils were asked was, "Do you think that being male or female makes a difference to your life generally in any way?" The basic response to this question was quite gendered. Approximately two-thirds of girls (thirty-two) answered yes, gender does make a difference, with a third (sixteen) saying that it does not make a difference, and two not providing specific responses. The boys' responses were much more evenly divided, with twenty-six arguing that gender does make a difference, and twenty-four claiming that it does not. There were no obvious differences in responses according to age, although when ethnicity was included in the analysis it became noticeable that a particularly large number of Afro-Caribbean year 11 boys said that gender does make a difference (nine) compared with those who said it did not (three). Also, the same number of Anglo year 10 girls (five) said that gender does not make a difference as those who said that it does. Of those who said gender does not make a difference to one's life, it was not always clear whether they simply thought that gender does not have an effect, or whether they believed that gender *should not* make a difference. For example, in the cases of a couple of the Anglo girls it became clear later in their interviews that they simply felt strongly that one's gender *should* not make a difference. Further, a large number of girls and boys argued that while gender used to make a difference to people's lives in the past, this is no longer the case. This supports the findings of Volman and Ten Dam (1998), who raise concerns that a discourse of equal opportunities among young people, which presents gender discrimination as a thing of the past, is blinding them to continuing gender inequality.

Young People's Discussion about Gender and Gender Discrimination

Of those pupils who claimed that gender makes a difference to one's life, the majority gave the world of adult work and employment as an example. Within these responses relating to the workplace, the two main explanations that pupils gave were gender discrimination against women (referred to by the majority of girls and some boys) and stereotypical or innate gender differences (referred to by a large proportion of the boys and a few girls). A further ten girls and one boy listed other types of sexism or discrimination against women apart from in employment. Finally, four girls and four boys mentioned discrimination against men, or female advantage, and discrimination against females, or separately. That girls articulate greater awareness of gender discrimination than do boys is supported by the findings of my study in primary school (Francis, 1997b; 1998a), which showed that approximately 80 per cent of girls and 60 per cent of boys claimed to have observed sexist incidents in school. There appear to be three possible reasons why more secondary school girls than boys raised gender discrimination as an issue affecting one's life. First, because gender discrimination tends to affect females more than males, boys may simply be less aware of the issue than are girls. Second, girls might expect an interview with a female researcher to be conducive to discussing discrimination against women, whereas boys might feel more defensive. This relates to the third possible reason: Billig et al. (1988) have argued that in Western society the discourse of democracy is so strong that to be seen to have an overt power advantage over others is often seen as an embarrassment. Consequently powerful groups often try to disguise their power advantage. For this reason boys (males) may be loath to recognize the potential advantage conferred to them by their sex via recognition of gender discrimination.

Besides discrimination in the workplace, several other types of gender discrimination were discussed by the pupils. One theme that recurred quite frequently among girls was the restrictions placed on them which they felt boys did not have to adhere to. For example, Jenny (Anglo, year 10) observes that parents treat boys and girls differently and are more worried about girls, consequently regulating them more carefully. Jenny notes that this is a difficult issue: she sympathizes with parents, pointing out that females are in danger of rape. This picks up on what I call the discourse of 'female fear': despite the fact that young men are actually more likely to be attacked outside the home than are young women, concerns about potential rape or sexual assault are taken on by girls from a very early age (Francis, 1998a). Hence Simone (Anglo, year 11) explains that unlike boys girls have to be careful when walking alone at night. Hazel (Middle-Eastern, year 10) also notes parents' protectiveness of girls, complaining that girls are not allowed to stay out late or do as many things as boys.

Tim (Afro-Caribbean, year 11) observes that some things are seen as 'boyish' or 'girlish', although he does not believe one's sex should make a difference to what one does. Maisie (Anglo, year 10) discusses what can happen if a girl *does* behave in the same way as a boy:

I: How about outside school, society more generally, do you think being male or female impacts on your life, makes a difference to your life in any [way?

M: [*Yeah*, erm (.) um, I suppose boys are (.), they're sort of allowed to get up to a lot more things than girls can, like '*specially*, things they're allowed to get away with (.) like, say erm you're at a party or whatever, boys are allowed to sort of go (.) to, to *do* things to girls that girls don't wanna do, and, like, boys are like branded like 'Yeah you've got that far', and girls are like '*you're* a–' er (.)

I: Slag

M: Yeah er, oh, yeah you are and I don't know why that is and that just *really annoys* me (.) but, boys just get away with a lot more, in general, than erm girls do, I think so

Hence doing things which girls are not supposed to (for instance, engaging in sexual activity) risks the penalty of being branded a slag, whereas boys are congratulated by their peers for the same behaviour. Justice (African, year 10) maintains that many boys (including his friends) do not think women are 'as good' as men, suggesting this discrimination as a way in which gender can affect one's life.

The other forms of discrimination that pupils mentioned were a lack of parental interest in girls and discrimination over activities. Regarding the latter, the main concern was the same one that I found in the primary school:

girls' exclusion from football. It is interesting to read the Adlers' (1998) accounts of playground activity in the United States, as girls, not boys, are involved in regular mass games of football ('soccer'). Yet here in Europe football remains perceived by the majority as a male domain, to the continuing frustration of many primary and secondary school girls. Serena's (Mediterranean, year 11) account captures the sense of injustice and real bitterness that many girls experience in relation to this issue:

S: Well, erm, I tell you what, I was in this school, and in primary school
      I played for the football team I was the only girl–
I: Mm
S: The, the whole year, like, the whole time I was there actually; and I
      come here [Sandyfields School] I asked to join the football team, they
      goes 'come to the try-outs' (.) an' *after*wards I was told by the, erm,
      PE teacher, 'oh you're, erm, 's good as half the boys there', which,
      you know, [made me pleased an' everything, I thought I was on the
      team (.)
I: [Mm
S: Next day, next time I went up to 'im, 'e goes 'No, you can't be on the
      team Serena', I goes, 'why's that?', an' 'e goes, 'you know, cos, erm,
      you might get *hurt*, these are *boys* now', {I laugh} an' 'e goes, I goes,
      'yeah, well I played with boys in primary school', [an' 'e goes {gruff
      voice}, 'yeah, but these are grown up men, you might get hurt, you
I: [Yeah
S: can come along an' cheer if you like' (.) {I tut} but, on *Saturdays*, this
      is how different attitudes are, I go to L Park every Saturday, I'm the
      only girl there, and I play with *men*, like *18 to 45* year olds and stuff

Finally, a further four boys and four girls provided examples of boys being discriminated against, or girls advantaged, because of their gender (the girls gave this suggestion along with other examples of discrimination against girls). Two boys maintained that females have an advantage because of the code that is supposed to put 'ladies first' and because (according to Craig, an Afro-Caribbean, year 11 boy) women can "get away with things" by "doing that women's thing, curl their hair or whatever they do". (Of course, this notion of women getting away with things by proverbially fluttering their eyelashes seems to assume that those with the power to penalize or reward them are heterosexual males!) Another explanation was the reported female orientation to schoolwork which advantaged girls. But four pupils (two boys and two girls) observed the way in which groups of boys are more likely to raise the suspicions of the police or security guards than are girls. Hence, Denzel (Afro-Caribbean, year 10) explains that gender does make a difference in the outside world in the following way:

D: It *does*, it does, a *big* difference, cos er (.) {sighs} *shops* an wh–, er, if you walk in, no, you, say I go in, like, Tescos, I could go in there with a bunch of boys, an' they all *follow us about*, you know? and I'm not a person who *steals*, *t'ieves*, causes *trouble*, I'm real far from trouble cos if I came 'trouble with the police I'd never see daylight again

I: Mm

D: So, I'm not a person who's looking for trouble, I'd rather stay *well away* from it, so *I'm* not going in there to trouble, it's just that, it's just *so irritating*, having a security guard following you about when you're not causing *no* harm, you know? (.) but when you see a bunch of *girls* in there you know, it's a bit different, the security guard lightens up, cos probably, I dunno, you know?

Denzel went on to talk about how this particularly affects black boys, and how shopkeepers seem to treat him and his black male friends with more suspicion than they do white boys. However, while this is quite likely to be the case, it seems from the findings of Pattman et al. (1998b) that this issue of distrust of male youths affects and is strongly resented by Anglo boys too. The boys' complaints illustrate the way in which society tends to view male youth as a problem. This has been the case ever since 'youth culture' came into being in the West in the second half of the twentieth century. It can be exemplified by the moral panics concerning mods and rockers in the 1960s (Cohen, 1973), vandalism in the 1980s and joy-riding in the 1990s. It is important that we (adults) do not to alienate boys by tarring all boys with the same brush, and that we bear in mind that only a small proportion of boys are involved in criminal activity, just as only some boys behave in 'laddish' ways in the classroom.

However, it was gender discrimination at work which most of the pupils alluded to when maintaining that gender makes a difference to one's life. This was particularly true of girls, of whom twenty-one raised the issue of discrimination against women in the workplace (compared with only six boys). It seems surprising that so many pupils referred to potential discrimination in employment. This issue might have been to some extent evoked by an earlier question in the interview schedule asking them what job they would like to do after leaving school or college. However, it also seems to indicate a strong concern with the future work environment on the part of these (particularly female) pupils.

Girls talked about the possibility of sexual harassment in the workplace, as well as discrimination in employment practice. There were three areas of concern regarding employment practice: pay, job allocation and ready employment. Concerning pay, Shanice (Afro-Caribbean, year 10) expressed the anxiety raised by a number of girls, confiding glumly, "I hear about women doing the same job as men but not getting the same amount of pay and all that? I hear about that, and I hear about all sex discrimination in the workplace". Shamilla (South Asian, year 10) also made this complaint, noting that race as well as gender can affect salary and promotion.

Girls were concerned about employers discriminating according to gender, both for certain types of occupation and for promotion to managerial positions. Regarding the latter issue, many pupils felt that employers often hold sexist preconceptions concerning women's abilities, expecting men to work harder, or "to do a little bit better" (as Dwight, Afro-Caribbean, year 11, puts it). This then affects women's promotion opportunities: Sabina (South Asian, year 10) explains, "If there's a guy and a girl you know working for a job they wanted then most probably the guy gets it". Calvin (Afro-Caribbean, year 11) agrees, "Some managerial jobs (.), um, a woman would *not* mostly be likely to get the job if a man applied for it". These findings lend support to the speculations of Benskin (1994) and Pickering (1997), who suggest that a possible explanation for girls' higher levels of motivation and achievement in the secondary school might be a feeling that they have to do better than boys in order to compete with them on even terms in the workplace. Certainly these girls and boys believed that where a woman and a man were equally able the man would be more likely to be selected for employment or promotion.

Many girls also drew on personal or anecdotal evidence to argue that there is still discrimination against women when attempting to enter traditionally masculine occupations. A number of girls had ready examples of sisters, cousins and the like who had attempted to get jobs traditionally seen as male, and who had been unsuccessful (although some had apparently persevered and had gone on to excel in these occupations). Professional football was raised again a number of times, in terms of women's exclusion from a footballing career. This issue may be particularly pertinent in London schools. Probably because of the proliferation of football clubs in London, a number of my male respondents were already playing semi-professional football. Eve (Afro-Caribbean, year 11) discussed her concerns that she might be discriminated against when attempting to pursue her chosen career as a pilot. However, manual and technical jobs (such as construction work) were those from which most girls suggested employers would attempt to exclude women.

This exclusion of women from 'labouring' work leads to the third area of job allocation in which some pupils felt females are disadvantaged: ready employment. A number of pupils maintained that it is easier for men to get jobs, particularly those jobs not requiring qualifications. Lucy (Anglo, year 11) explains:

I: That's interesting
A: Yeah

Girls' View of Career and Career Access

Very little has been said about the reasons for the improvement in the educational achievement of girls. What little speculation there is has usually either focused on the apparent success of equal opportunities programmes or on the stress on coursework for GCSE assessment. (The argument being that girls are better at written presentation and less good at exams. However, as was observed in Chapter 1, girls' continued success despite the recent reduction in coursework at GCSE level, is not explained by this argument.) The explanation I am suggesting is clearly very different from both these arguments. Arnot et al. (1999) make the more general argument that economic and social change (the latter including the impact of feminism) have impacted on girls' educational achievement. Although recognizing the greater career ambition of many contemporary schoolgirls, they maintain that this factor is unlikely on its own to explain girls' improved educational performance. Economic and social change explains girls' increased ambition concerning their careers. Yet I am suggesting this increased ambition, coupled with a feeling that opportunities in the workplace are skewed against them, is what has provided girls with new motivation for achievement at school. Of course, any assertion that girls work particularly hard at school because they see themselves as disadvantaged in the workplace supposes two things. First, that girls want jobs and see their future employment as important. Second, that girls believe success at school will help them to gain employment. This section reports findings from the study which go some way to answering these questions.

When asked what job they wanted to do when they completed their education, girls listed thirty-six different jobs and boys listed thirty-three. Seven girls and thirteen boys listed more than one job. The diversity of jobs chosen by pupils, particularly girls, supports my findings in the primary school that girls now consider a far wider range of occupations than reported in studies in the early 1980s (Francis, 1996). Moreover, whereas Spender (1982) and others found that secondary school girls largely aspired to stereotypically feminine, non-professional jobs, I found that thirty girls (nearly two-thirds) chose jobs that normally require a degree. Only sixteen chose jobs that did not require a degree (four did not know what occupation they wished to pursue). This trend was even stronger among the boys, with thirty-five choosing jobs that usually require a degree. This finding suggests, then, that boys' comparative underperformance at secondary school level cannot be explained by a lack of career ambition. Hence it questions the argument made by Pickering (1997) and a number of my pupil respondents that boys (naively) assume that they will get manual jobs on entering the workplace. On the other hand, my research was conducted with pupils from upper- and middle-ability streams; perhaps such assumptions could be expected to be more prominent among boys in the lowest stream.

Yet it is the case that over the last 20 years girls' career aspirations have dramatically altered. Whereas Spender (1982), Gaskell (1992) and others found girls preparing to work until they were married, and then to stop work or assume the role of secondary breadwinner, my findings in the primary and secondary school show that girls are now far more career oriented. The majority appear to see their chosen careers as reflecting their identity rather than viewing paid work as a stopgap before marriage (see also Riddell, 1992; Sharpe, 1994). This may be partly the result of equal opportunities programmes and a larger availability of role models as increasing numbers of women participate in, and succeed in, the labour market. However, it may also stem from changes in society that have brought a new materialism and realism. The increasing divorce rate and the number of single-parent families seemed to have had an impact on the thinking of some girls in my primary school study, who argued that women must fend for themselves as you 'cannot rely on a man' (Francis, 1998a). Moreover, in two-parent families it is now far more usual for both parents to work, even full-time, than was the case even a decade ago.

Many of the girls' career choices were exceedingly ambitious. The most frequently listed job was doctor, chosen by six girls. Three girls said "doctor", and three others specified "paediatrician" (probably reflecting the influence of contemporary TV shows such as *Casualty* and *ER*). Joint second, with four votes each, were solicitor (or "lawyer", as the job tends to be referred to by pupils) and actor. Traditional choices, such as hairdresser, nurse, air hostess and clerical worker, did feature, but only got one vote each. Moreover, traditionally masculine occupations, such as soldier, business person, computer scientist, mathematician and banker, were also chosen by girls. Riddell (1992) also found that girls are increasingly willing to consider non-traditional career paths. These choices seem to illustrate the diversity in girls' aspirations, and the way in which many see a whole spectrum of roles as being potentially appropriate for them.

Boys were generally more conservative: only three of their choices could be seen as traditionally feminine (counsellor, social worker and teacher), and, of these, two were chosen by the same boy. This greater conservatism of boys concerning gender and career is consistent with the findings of previous research[1] and lends support to the argument that boys are less willing to experiment in transgressing traditional gender positions than are girls (Pickering, 1997). The most popular career for boys was professional footballer: this was chosen by eight boys. This is not necessarily so unrealistic a choice as it might first appear: as I noted above, a number of boys in the study were already playing semi-professional football or had agents. However, may of the boys that listed footballer as a chosen career also listed another job as well as a fall-back to football, demonstrating a healthy realism. Despite their success at football, some boys, such as Paul (Anglo, year 11) and Will (Afro-Caribbean, year 11), explained their determination to go to college in case their football careers do not take off or are cut short. The second most popular occupations among the boys were solicitor and business person, both of which were chosen by five boys.

Despite the diversity in choice of occupation expressed by both male and female pupil groups, and the evident readiness to explore new options on the part of some of the girls particularly, on closer analysis I still found broadly gendered trends in these choices. As with my analysis of primary school children's future job choices (Francis, 1996), I found that a gender dichotomy was evident, with girls tending to opt for artistic or 'caring' professions, and boys opting for occupations that were scientific, technical or business oriented. For example, twenty-seven of the boys' and only seven of the girls' choices could be described as exclusively scientific, technical or business oriented; twenty-two jobs chosen by girls and twelve chosen by boys could be described as exclusively artistic or 'caring'. This trend is of course demonstrated by the continuing high numbers of young women choosing arts and humanities courses, and young men choosing science courses, at 'A' level and degree level, and the larger proportion of young men who take up vocational training. However, this difference in the types of courses and jobs pursued by male and female pupils does not detract from the main point regarding my earlier argument: that the majority of girls were found to be ambitious concerning their future work, aspiring to 'careers' rather than 'jobs'. It is arguable, then, that if they seriously seek such careers, yet see the adult workplace as being gender-discriminatory, they might expect to have to invest in means of decreasing their gender disadvantage by increasing their likelihood of resisting employer discrimination. In terms of education, such investments or weapons might be knowledge and experience, and qualifications.

In fact, my findings show that virtually all pupils, both male and female, believed that participation in further education is important, mainly because of the qualifications that it provides one with. Over 90 per cent of pupils said that further education is important, and 98 per cent said that they intended to pursue it after leaving secondary school. These figures are exceedingly high and may partly be explained by the geographical location of the study: Department of Education and Employment figures (1998a) show that a particularly high proportion of London pupils participate in further education and training. It became clear that six main discourses predominated among secondary pupils regarding further education. These were, 'The importance of being educated' (which stressed the value of education in its own right); 'The developmental usefulness of education' (which presented education as providing one with the knowledge and the experience to make informed decisions); 'The status and value of post-16 education and qualifications'; 'Meritocracy' (here suggesting that further education would get one a good job); 'Competition' (presenting the world of employment as a 'jungle', where qualifications would help one gain advantage); and 'Hard Times' (which stressed the high levels of youth unemployment and disenfranchisement).

These discourses often overlapped. It is the last four discourses that particularly concern us here. Besides the gender discrimination that many girls believed to permeate the adult workplace, many pupils were aware of the high levels of youth unemployment. Using the discourses of 'hard times' and 'competition', they presented the world of employment as being hard and competitive, 'a jungle', often alluding to apparently rosier times when it was easier for young people to find work. In this environment, qualifications provided by further or higher education were seen as insurance or as an investment. When I asked what difference further education makes, Joseph (Afro-Caribbean, year 10) explains that, "Without further education you'll probably end up working in *Sains*burys". Pupils argued that one needed further education qualifications in order to secure a 'good' job. Indeed, a number of pupils argued that one needed such qualifications in order to secure *any* job. Maisie (Anglo, year 10) explains:

I: Do you think further education's important?

M: Ye:ah, cos, um, like, specially the way things are going at the moment, with, um, sort of, employment and that you 'ave to 'ave good grades and that to get, like, *just a job* really

I: Mm

M: So many people doing college and everything you've got to start keeping up with them otherwise {I laugh} you won't get a job

Thus Maisie's statement reflects the discourses of 'hard times', the status and value of post-16 education and qualifications, and competition.

In terms of pupils' talk about further education, there were few clear gender differences. Pupils mainly said it was important, and 98 per cent of pupils said that they intended to pursue it. Male and female pupils drew on a discourse of meritocracy to suggest that investment in further education qualifications would help one to gain an advantage in the competitive jobs market. (As Adam, Anglo, year 11, explains, "the more education the more you get paid really, in my opinion anyway".) However, remembering the high proportion of girls that said gender discrimination exists in the adult workplace, and particularly in employment practices, it does not appear unreasonable to suggest that girls in particular may see the gaining of qualifications as imperative for securing their future careers. Indeed, although I did not ask pupils specifically whether they intended to continue to university after further education, many pupils voluntarily talked about their university aspirations, and of these a higher proportion were female (thirty-two girls compared with twenty boys). Of course, had I asked all pupils whether they planned to go to university, it is possible that more boys might have said "yes", but the enthusiasm for higher education that girls expressed in their talk (coupled with the fact that women do now enter British higher education in slightly greater numbers than do men) seems to lend some credence to my argument. Whether girls' investment in their futures does in fact pay off is debatable. As Rees (1999) observes, men still hold the vast majority of top jobs across Europe, although women have increasingly broken into middle-management. Moreover, the different types of post-16 courses and careers pursued by men and women mean that particularly highly remunerated or high status jobs continue to go to men. In this sense, the girls' fears about future gender disadvantage in the workplace, and male complacency about the future, appear to be justified. Work needs to be done in schools to show pupils of both sexes the current and developing patterns of job availability and skill shortage, and the way in which their choices of course and career can influence their future career prospects. This issue will be returned to in Chapter 9.

To summarize, this chapter has shown how the majority of girls, and many of their male counterparts, still say that one's gender affects one's life in various ways. All of their observations deserve consideration from us as educationalists and parents, be it the ways girls feel their lives are more closely regulated and protected than boys (particularly by parents), or the ways in which boys feel victimized and problematized (particularly by teachers, the police, security guards, etc.). However, the most frequently noted impact of gender was in the area of employment, and what the pupils (particularly girls) saw as the gender-discriminatory nature of the adult workplace. That twenty-one of the fifty girls in the study raised this topic spontaneously illustrates the level of concern among girls over this issue. I have attempted to relate girls' recent success at GCSE level and increasing educational success generally to this finding concerning their view of the adult workplace. Showing that girls are now far more ambitious concerning their future careers than was the case 20 years ago, I have suggested that girls attach particular importance to their educational achievement as an investment with which to combat any disadvantage they might face as a result of discrimination in the employment market.

It is true that boys were equally ambitious in terms of their careers and also placed a high importance on further education in the belief that qualifications would earn them better jobs. However, my main point is that girls' similar preoccupation with qualifications and careers marks a *change* for girls. It may be this change in their post-secondary-school aspirations which partly explains their swift acceleration in achievement at GCSE level, and their increasing continuation to higher education. Moreover, their awareness of the issue of workplace discrimination may provide them with an extra spur in their efforts in education, which does not apply to boys. Finally, drawing on the findings from the previous chapter, it is also arguable that educational achievement does not sit so uneasily with girls' dominant constructions of femininity as it does with many boys' constructions of masculinity. This point will be explored further in the next chapter.

7 Young People's Talk about Gender and Behaviour

Classroom observation showed that although there was as much diversity of behaviour within gender groups as there was between genders; in general, there were also clear tendencies of difference in the classroom behaviour of boys and girls. More boys than girls were loud and disruptive, and boys tended to monopolize the classroom space. Chapter 3 discussed how the symbolic masculine culture was maintained among boys in the classroom via physical aggression and dominance, verbal aggression and banter (including the use of homophobic and misogynist abuse), and an interest in gender-typed pastimes. Chapter 4 added that many boys tend to construct themselves as 'having a laugh' in the classroom, in order to gain or maintain social status with their peers. Looking at these findings, it seems that, as Salisbury and Jackson (1996), Younger and Warrington (1996), Skelton (1997) and Pickering (1997) have argued, many boys are taking up a particular strategy for constructing their masculinity in the classroom, and that this construction is at odds with the school ethos. Salisbury and Jackson have labelled this particular masculine persona 'macho'. I have opted to use the label 'laddish' instead, because machismo tends to evoke physical strength and aggression: this did not always seem part of the construction taken up by, for example, class clowns. Indeed, the disruption and resistance of many of these boys was based on wit and silliness rather than overt aggression. The term 'laddish' incorporates both aspects.

The concept of the 'lad' requires some explanation. The term has been traditionally used to describe boys or young men and has gradually taken on a particular meaning around the notion of a male being 'one of the lads'. This term evokes a young, exclusively male, group, and the hedonistic practices popularly associated with such groups (for example 'having a laugh', disruptive behaviour, objectifying women, alcohol consumption, and an interest in pastimes and subjects constructed as masculine). The term was famously used in a sociological study by Paul Willis in the 1970s to describe a group of white, working-class, anti-school boys (Willis, 1977).

The term 'lads' tended to imply working-class, white youths. However, in the 1990s a backlash against 'political correctness' led to a defiant resurgence of traditional 'laddish' values in the media, typified by the men's magazine *Loaded* and the popular sit-com *Men Behaving Badly*. The values of 'lads' were appropriated by and popularized for middle class (and often middle-aged) men, and the term has gained a new prominence in popular and media culture.

Given the recent media furore over the apparent 'underachievement' of boys in schools, and the frequent pronouncements on the issue by prominent figures such as Chris Woodhead (Chief Inspector for Schools and Colleges), it is not surprising that 'boys' underachievement' has been the focus of recent government attention. Besides having introduced new initiatives intended to make learning attractive to boys (e.g. Department of Education and Employment, 1998b), the attitudes of boys to learning have been criticized by ministers. In a speech at the 11th International Conference for School Effectiveness and Improvement, the then Schools Standards Minister, Stephen Byers, actually used the term 'laddish' to describe boys' behaviour in school. He argued that boys' 'laddish' anti-school attitudes were impeding their progress at school (*The Guardian*, 1998). This kind of critical comment, placing the responsibility for 'boys' underachievement' with boys themselves, marks a distinct discursive shift. Epstein et al. (1998) point out that commentary on the issue of 'boys' underachievement' has typically drawn on discourses of 'poor boys', which blame schools, teachers, feminists and/or teaching and examination practices for boys' underachievement compared with girls. Yet now blame was apparently being reassigned to boys themselves. This may be part of a more general discursive shift propagated by the New Labour government, which focuses on individual responsibility (for example for maintaining a stable family environment, for taking care of one's own future financial security, for ensuring that one has the required and updated skills and qualifications required in the labour market, and so on). Sampson (1989) argued that such discourses of individuality conveniently pathologize 'failing' individuals, locating the fault in individuals while concealing contributing social factors.

This chapter examines pupils' responses to Byers' argument concerning schoolboys and achievement. My final interview question reported Byers' statement about boys' behaviour and asked pupils to respond to it.[1] Their opinions are analysed in order to explore their constructions of gender and behaviour in the classroom.

Byers' criticism of boys' laddish attitudes was controversial. His claim that such attitudes were damaging the achievements of boys was denounced by the then editor of the *Independent* newspaper, who maintained that the government should be concentrating on raising standards for all rather than attempting cultural analysis (cited in Griffin, 1998). However, this chapter will show that many secondary school pupils themselves considered Byers' perception of boys and their behaviour to be justified.

In the following discussion the various discourses that pupils drew upon in their constructions of boys' behaviour in school will be analysed. As I described in Chapter 2, I have found the concept of discourse invaluable for two reasons. It explains the contradictory positions and expressions that people produce in interaction and also the way in which people's power positions shift and change when interacting with others.

Numerical Analysis

A total of sixty-seven (67 per cent) pupils agreed with Byers' claim that the 'laddish' behaviour of boys is impeding their learning. Of these, thirty-five were girls (70 per cent) and thirty-two were boys (64 per cent). Only just over a quarter of pupils (27 per cent) disagreed, with 6 per cent of pupils saying that they did not know, or they did not respond directly to the question. In categorizing the responses as agreeing, only those whose first response was "yes", or "that's true" have been included in the figure (so we can see that the representation of two-thirds agreeing is the most conservative interpretation: had I included those who said that it was true of *some* boys, or those who had initially responded that Byers' statement was false but had later changed their minds, the figure would have been higher still). Many pupils who initially responded that Byers' statement was untrue later went on to say that some boys do behave 'laddishly', but that it is not true of all boys. Some of the pupils who replied that it is true also qualified their statements with the point that it is not true of *all* boys. However, even of the 27 per cent who disagreed, more said that some boys did behave 'laddishly' than said that Byers' view was entirely misplaced.

The balance of responses was similar between schools, and similar proportions of girls agreed with Byers' argument in years 10 and 11. However, boys in year 11 were more likely to agree than were their year 10 counterparts: almost half of year 10 boys disagreed with Byers' statement. There were also differences according to ethnicity: the two groups in which the largest proportions supported Byers' statement were Afro-Caribbean girls (nine of ten), and Anglo boys (twelve of fifteen). I cannot think of obvious reasons for these patterns, although perhaps in the case of Anglo boys the fact that 'laddism' has traditionally been applied to people of their race and gender may have led to a greater level of association.

The pupils who agreed with Byers' claim that the 'laddish' behaviour of boys is impeding their learning were asked why boys were behaving in this way. There were fourteen different explanations for boys' 'laddish' behaviour, and these are discussed separately here in order to analyse the supporting discourses that pupils drew upon in their discussion of the behaviour of boys. We begin with the arguments supported by the greatest numbers of pupils. Many pupils gave more than one explanation during the course of their discussion of Byers' comments; thus the figures provided simply record the number of times a reason was suggested by pupils.

In looking at the pupils' arguments, it is important to remember the peculiar position in which my male respondents were placed in relation to this question about 'laddish' behaviour. A female interviewer was in effect asking them to analyse the behaviour of themselves and their male peers in relation to a pejorative statement. Many of the boys distanced themselves from 'other boys' whom they depicted as acting in this manner. Others declared participation in such behaviour. Their talk about their own laddish behaviour was usually good-humouredly sheepish, but some did not appear to relate pejorative connotations to the term 'lad' at all, even in an educational environment. For example, I unintentionally offended Ron (mixed-race, year 10) in my efforts not to label him:

I: The ex-Education Minister Stephen Byers said that boys' *laddish behaviour* is stopping them doing well at school, what do you think about that?

R: (.) *Na:ah*, cos there's nuff, there's *enough* people I hang round with, and they don't, they don't exactly *act like me*, cos I'm, I'm in quite a bit of trouble at the moment, but=

I: Can I just hold you there?

R: Yeh

I: Are you saying that you, behave in a laddish way?

R: {apparently surprised at my question} Yeh

I: Right, {laughing} okay (.) right, cos I wouldn't *assume* that, you know=

R: *Why*?

I: Mm?

R: What do you mean?

I: Well I hadn't *taken that for granted*, I hadn't thought of *you* as a laddish person, [but if you're saying you *are* laddish, that's fine

R: [What (.) what do you mean?, what you think I'm *feminine*?

I: *No* (.) not, certainly not, no, but what I mean is I didn't want to put that *definition* on you=

R: {relieved} Oh right

I: =So I'm just checking that you *are* putting that definition on *yourself*

R: Oh right, *ye:ah*

boring and superficial. From this perspective, girls only engage so effectively with schoolwork because they have *nothing better to do*.

The Greater Maturity of Girls

The issue of male immaturity was raised again in response to Byers' statement on boys' behaviour. This explanation for boys' laddish behaviour bears some relation to that of innate gender differences (see below), as it also relates boys' behaviour to biology. Pupils argued that girls mature more quickly than boys, and that this is reflected in classroom behaviour. However, the narrative differed in that it did not present these gender differences as fixed: boys will grow out of their disruptive behaviour. As Leticia (mixed race, year 10) explained,

L: (.) Cos I think, cos girls are more mature than boys, girls mature faster than boys?

I: Right

L: And they just take a bit more time, so they act more immature

I: So you think they'll grow out of it?

L: {laughing} Event*ually*

Gemma (Anglo, year 11) shared this interpretation, but is rather less tolerant of boys' 'immaturity', saying of Byers' statement, "I think sometimes it *is true* cos boys (.) don't grow up as quick as girls (.) an' some of 'em should still be in year *8* cos they start *cussing girls* an' that, and hardly any of ' em get on with their work". The implicitly (or in the case of Gemma and others, explicitly) pejorative element in the construction of boys as maturing more slowly than girls may explain why girls were slightly more likely to use the argument than were boys. Six girls and four boys used this argument.

Gemma went on to link boys' immaturity to their overconcern to 'act tough' or impress their friends, and this link was evident in a number of girls' transcripts. For example, Sau-Wah (East Asian, year 10) maintained that girls do not tease one another about working hard so much as boys do because they are more mature. Thus the immaturity of the boys was usually presented as manifesting itself in the laddish behaviour. However, Will (Afro-Caribbean, year 11) explained this differently, arguing that it is the immaturity of some boys which prevents them from realizing that they should be concentrating on schoolwork rather than engaging in laddish behaviour, "they're not *mature* enough to, you know, they don't want to capitalize on the, opportunity that they *have*, to, you know, progress forward".

Innate Differences between Genders

Some pupils suggested that boys' laddish classroom behaviour is due to natural, innate differences between the genders. Calvin (Afro-Caribbean, year 11) illustrated this position when he argued that, "The girls are more focused on the work than the boys", and suggests {laughing} "It must be something in their genes or somethink". Daniel (Afro-Caribbean, year 10) maintained that boys like to act 'hard' to impress girls; yet when I asked him why, in that case, girls do not have to act hard to impress the boys he replied, "Don't know, don't know what's in a girl's mind […] {to me, as a 'girl'} *You're* going to have to answer that question". Here the genders are presented as so separate that Daniel cannot be expected to attempt to envisage what might motivate a female. Hence such arguments drew on a discourse of innate inequality between genders, which I identified in my work in primary school (Francis, 1998a; 1999c). However, whereas in the primary school this discourse was usually drawn on to support narratives of male superiority and differences in ability, here it was being used to explain differences in behaviour.

This explanation of innate gender differences was used by six boys and only one girl. Mahony (1998) also found that 'biological accounts' of gender were frequently used by boys, often in order to argue that gender differences are inevitable. My data support her argument, because, as well as using this argument more than did girls, a number of the boys drew on this discourse of innate inequality between genders to avert responsibility for disruptive behaviour. Adam (Anglo, year 11) responded to Byers' argument by saying, "Yes, {laughing} that's *very true* as it goes, yeah, cos, I dunno, boys are boys really ain't they?". Thus he echoed the 'boys will be boys' narrative which Epstein et al. (1998) identify as excusing boys in the 'boys' educational failure' debate.

Wishing to Impress Girls

Four boys and two girls maintained that boys behave laddishly in order to impress (and consequently attract) girls. However, the majority of pupils who suggested a wish to impress girls as an explanation of boys' laddish behaviour did so alongside other suggestions. Only one of the boys, Anthony (Afro-Caribbean, year 10) explained boys' behaviour solely in these terms, saying of Byers' argument, "Yeh I do *believe* that, cos most boys like to impress the girls they like in the class". Joseph (Afro-Caribbean, year 10) also linked laddishness and 'hardness' to attracting girls:

J: Well they [boys] all wanna be like, strong, and act, act, people are strong right, in a sense, and hang around with girls a lot, {I laugh} at least, not hang around with girls, but erm *go out* with girls, and stuff (.) erm, things like that make people wanna *fight* more

I: (.) So you think that (.) so you think that the boys concerned think that by being, hard, being strong=

J: Yeh

I: They're gonna attract a woman more?

J: Mm-hm {nods}

I: And do you think that's true or not?

J: (.) Well, er, in *my* age group, think it's true, but when they come up, can move on, just–

I: Right, right that's interesting (.) what about the girls in your class, I mean do you think they're *all* impressed by hard men or not?

J: Not *really*

Yet while Joseph hesitantly concluded that not all the girls in his class are attracted to 'hard men', Maisie (Anglo, year 10) admitted that some girls may be implicated in the perpetuation of laddish behaviour by being attracted to such boys. Sandra (Anglo, year 10) agreed that "girls tend to go for, you know more loudish people than the people who just sit quietly and do their work", because they "think it's cool" to be with such a person. This is an important point for feminist reflection, for it suggests that some girls are helping to perpetuate the laddish behaviour criticized by so many other girls in my study. It also ties in with the point I made in Chapter 4, that I and some of the teachers (male and female) found some laddish boys particularly appealing. Perhaps females are attracted to macho, laddish boys because they represent the 'other', all that is oppositional to femininity, so strongly: girls are discouraged and discourage themselves from behaving in these traditionally masculine ways, and consequently project their desire for such behaviour into attraction to laddish males. A further explanation is simply that because these boys are expressing what society values in men (strength, daring, wit, resistance, etc.), it makes them particularly socially acceptable and hence attractive. Whatever the reason, this point has some bearing on the boys' underachievement debate, and will be discussed further in the following chapters.

Female Keenness and Willingness to Work Hard

This narrative tended to depict boys' laddish behaviour as illuminated by comparisons with girls' studious and learning-oriented behaviour. For example, Daniel (Afro-Caribbean, year 10) argues that "girls learn, the, they're more willing to learn than boys". This narrative was used by five boys and only one girl. Even this girl couched her argument around criticism of the boys' disruptive behaviour, and only alluded to girls' industry once when she said that while boys 'mess about', "girls they, um, they carry on working". Boys were more explicit about female enthusiasm or willingness to work, suggesting that this narrative was used as an excuse by boys: it is not so much that boys' laddish behaviour is wrong, but that girls are so studious. In this sense the narrative of female keenness and willingness to work hard might be seen to tie in with the argument maintaining that boys face more distractions than girls, positioning girls as overly studious and boring. Phoenix et al. (forthcoming) found that many boys admired girls' apparent focus on their schoolwork. Such admiration was occasionally evident among the boys in this study. However, it appeared that in some cases pupils were drawing on this narrative of female keenness in order to abdicate responsibility for male behaviour.

That Boys are More Competitive

That Boys like to 'Show off' and Seek Attention

These two arguments were closely related in pupil's talk about laddish behaviour. Two boys and two girls claimed that boys are more competitive than are girls, and that this leads them to behave in particular ways. In considering Byers' argument about laddish behaviour, Henderson (Afro-Caribbean, year 11) reflected,

H: Yeh (3) I think it could be *true* you know (.) boys like to, like, have a show at times, y'know, when it comes to work they wanna, be on top, and like, I think, *I* think he's right, in a way, because they like to, like, be *first* at everythink, and, like, be number one at everythink, [so like=

I: [But wouldn't that make them work *harder*, you'd think?

H: Well, some boys, they, they, some people take different roads, some people just wanna be on top of the class, a, answer all of the questions and then some boys just wanna be like, all [...] 'I can play football, I can be a real sportsman', other boys just like er 'oh I've got the looks I can get any girl' {I laugh} and all that=

I: {laughing} Okay, so they're competitive in, you can be the strongest, or [the best at=

H: [Or the best, yeah–

I: =sports, or the best womanizer, [or the best at learning?

H: [Yeah (.) Yeah

Henderson's comments support the findings of Mac an Ghaill (1994), Skelton (1997) and Sewell (1997) that boys adopt different strategies for 'doing' masculinity.

A further three girls and one boy simply argued that boys' laddish behaviour was caused by boys' penchant for attention seeking and/or 'showing off'. This explanation appeared linked with notions of boys' immaturity: Samantha (Anglo, year 10) made this explicit when she maintains that boys "like to show off" because they are "more immature". These arguments drew on a combination of female superiority, innate gender differences, and stereotypically gendered characteristics and behaviour discourses.

That Girls are More Worried about their Future Job Prospects and so Must Work Harder

That Boys take their Ability to Find Work in the Future for Granted

Again, these two explanations concerning future work were often interrelated and so are discussed together. Two boys and one girls made the former argument, maintaining that girls are more concerned about their future career prospects than are boys and hence work harder for their qualifications. Addi (African, year 11) argued that girls are more 'serious' than boys at school because, "boys think, 'Well, if I leave school, I can always get a job' and that, but the girls are, more *concerned*, about what they want to achieve". He explains, "the *girls*, when they *know* that, when, by the time they grow up yeah?, when they finish school, go to college, university (.) they'll need to support their *family* as well (.) but I mean the males just think they can get any job". This view that boys in turn were not working hard at school because of complacent expectations concerning future jobs was supported by other pupils (two boys and two girls). Anthony (Afro-Caribbean, year 10) argued, "Er, *most* boys don't care about school, cos (.) like, they know they can just go, go get a builder's job, physical (.) but *girls*, they've got to *work* for it, cos mostly I think they lack, power". Similarly, Jenny (Anglo, year 10) speculated that boys are not concerned about their grades because, "they think 'oh no, I'll go and be a carpenter, or I'll get a trade', or something like that".

These arguments support the idea that girls feel they have to be better than boys in order to compete on the same terms in the jobs market. Evidence presented in the previous chapter supports these suggestions, showing that many girls are acutely aware of, and concerned about, the issues of gender discrimination in the workplace and employment practices. On the other hand, again we have some pupils presenting boys as complacent and believing that they will inevitably find a job. As Pickering (1997) has observed, this assumption is no longer guaranteed. Not only are there more women competing with men for jobs in the workplace but also the unskilled manual jobs traditionally available to men with few qualifications are in increasingly short supply as the economic environment alters. However, as we saw in the last chapter, there is little evidence from my findings to support this view of boys as relying on the availability of manual work: boys were shown to perceive further education as important and were as ambitious as girls concerning their aspirations for professional careers. Yet there also appeared a suggestion in the talk of these pupils that boys are less concerned with planning and thinking about the future than are girls: boys were portrayed as hedonistic and living for the present (see Sewell, 1998). Susan (Anglo, year 11) encapsulated this perspective in her statement, "I think they [boys] just wanna have *fun* while they're this age, and they don't really think about the future".

Parental Influences on Boys

One boy argued that some fathers are still sexist and give their sons the impression that there will always be jobs for men irrespective of qualifications, with the result that their sons cease to bother with their schoolwork. Another boy suggested that boys' macho behaviour was influenced by their paternal role models, as he had noticed that it is usually fathers who discipline their children. Hence, as with the pupils who explained the laddish behaviour of boys' as being due to peer pressure, these boys used a social explanation.

Socio-cultural Expectations of Boys

A social explanation was also used less specifically by two girls, who simply said that boys behaved laddishly because that is what is expected of them.

Women's Liberation

During their discussion of Byers' comments, two girls used women's emancipation to explain girls' outperformance of boys at school. Sauria (South Asian, year 11) mused, "Um (.) I think girls (.) cos all, how girls were oppressed and women oppressed, I think that's made them, like, *come up* more and more determined to like *rule* the world, women power, all that rubbish, {I laugh and Sauria laughs too} all that rubbish, it's just made them, it's made them wanna be like men really, it's made them wanna race with men (.) they were like, sort of like, *hidden away*, they stayed in the home, kitchen, but *now* they're just trying to get out of it, run with the men basically". Donna (Afro-Caribbean, year 11) explained the recent reversal in gendered performance at secondary level in the following way:

D: Better than, I think that's because, boys used to dominate girls then (.) more
I: So what's changed?
D: Girls are becoming more independent now, they wanna do things for *themselves*, I mean, they don't wanna depend, depending on boys, they wanna go out, find their own job, earn their own money, stuff like that, girls are just more independent now in the last couple of years
I: Right (.) so it's the girls that are changing, and boys are staying the same, [basically?
D: [Yeah (.) cos they never really used to *give* girls a chance (.) like, really far far back it was expected that girls didn't even need an education they were just supposed to sit at home cooking whatever, but nowadays they wanna do their *own* thing

As I noted in the previous chapter, in my previous study I found evidence among primary school girls that changes in economic and social conditions and the ensuing trends, such as the increase in women engaging in paid work, and the increasing divorce rate, were affecting girls' expectations of their future lives (Francis, 1998a). Primary school girls often informed me that they expected to have careers *and* raise children, sometimes adding that one cannot rely on men. Such a narrative of female independence and self-sufficiency can be seen in Donna's argument. However, the notion of women having been 'kept in the kitchen' in 'olden times' (usually meaning before the 1990s), but having liberated themselves and gained equality of opportunity, is also evident in both girls' statements. This discourse of equal opportunity has been observed among secondary school children by Volman and Ten Dam (1998), who raise a concern that this discourse masks current gender inequalities, leading girls to believe that gender discrimination is a thing of the past and not related to their lives.

The Explanations of those who Disagreed with Byers' Claim

This section explores the arguments made by pupils who disagreed with Byers' statement that boys' laddish behaviour is impeding their learning. Some pupils simply disagreed with Byers about the *impact* of boys' behaviour. For example, Lynda (Anglo, year 10) said that the boys do 'mess around' in class, but that they still get their homework done, so it does not prevent them from learning. (She does however suggest that the behaviour of these boys can prevent *others* from learning.) Other pupils simply pointed out that there are academically oriented boys and that Byers is making a generalization based on the behaviour of a certain group of boys. Joseph (Afro-Caribbean, year 10) pointed out that "He hasn't met *all* the boys", explaining that just a "handful" of boys are persuaded by peer pressure to behave in the way Byers suggests. Oliver (East Asian, year 10) agrees that Byers' argument is "completely *stupid*", pointing out that plenty of boys are work-oriented.

Hence a large proportion of the pupils who disagreed with Byers' suggestion did so because they argued that although some boys did behave in laddish ways this was not the case with all boys. (This point was of course supported by my classroom observation). Luke (mixed race, year 11) argued this latter position, but his argument is particularly interesting as he went on to argue the benefits of the laddish behaviour expressed by some boys:

I: Um, the ex-Education Minister Stephen Byers said that boys' *laddish behaviour* was stopping them doing well at school, what do you think about that?

L: {chuckles} That ain't true (.) [boys=

I: [D–, yeh, go on (.)

L: It is *partly* true, but it's only like a small minority of boys, but they, like, [.] a lot of things, like, sometimes, it's like it's just the comedians, you only get *one* in the *class*, which without *them* the class wouldn't be like *in*teresting it'd be *bor*ing and everything (.) and no-one would be able to work properly, so you *need* that little bit of– (.)

I: So you're saying that it's only a *tiny* minority

L: Yeh

I: Yeah?, well, *with* that tiny minority would you say that it normally is a boy, when you talk about the classroom comedian, or can it be girls as well?

L: (.) Erm, it *can* be girls, but it's often specially boys

Luke's observations serve as an important reminder of the investments that pupils have in the expression of laddish behaviour in the classroom: this behaviour on the part of some pupils can provide entertainment for other pupils, and embody resistance, in what is often experienced by pupils as a monotonous and disempowering school regime. As such, this laddish behaviour also endows the boy(s) concerned with status among their peers.

Other pupils' explanations for their disagreement with Byers' view reflected discourses of equal opportunity and of individuality, which I also found being commonly used by primary school children (Francis, 1998a; 1999c). The equal opportunity narrative was conceived in the same way as the arguments of women's liberation that were used to support Byers' claim (see above). Pupils argued that 'these days' the genders are equal and that there are no differences in behaviour between girls and boys, often suggesting that Byers' view is based on his outdated memories of school. When Mohammed (African, year 11) is asked about Byers' claim, he replied, "probably in his day, but not now"; and Raymond (African, year 10) said that Byers is thinking of 'olden times'. Raymond maintains that girls are now girls behaving in 'macho' ways as well. Indeed, equality of behaviour was sometimes stressed. Marcus (Afro-Caribbean, year 11) maintained that, "now we're coming into the nineties [sic], like (.) boys and girls are really like becoming the *same*". He pointed out that, "Girls getting good at basketball, football (.) just the same, n' we are, boys are getting good at, *ballet*, aerobics"; he concluding that, "Everyone's just kind of, *equal*".

This notion that the genders are becoming more similar was articulated by a number of pupils. However, those who talked about this in more detail did not necessarily present an apparent increasing androgyny as unproblematic. Joseph's (Afro-Caribbean, year 10) interview provides a good example for discussion. He began by arguing that women are becoming "more male-ish" and that men are becoming more feminine, using a male friend's obsession with his looks and personal grooming as an example of boys taking on traditionally feminine behaviour. He also reflected that girls appear to become 'adult-like' earlier than boys and that girls at secondary school can be very 'hard': "there's girls in my class, right? Now I fear *them*, more than most boys in the school, yeah, those girls, if you really get on their nerves like, they'll most probably knock you out". He expressed some confusion and anxiety at this state of affairs, explaining that where one once had to worry which boy was "gonna beat the shit out of you.... Now you've got one of those girls gonna beat the shit out of you, {I laugh} no longer boys". He went on to explain his puzzlement that girls seem to mature and grow more quickly than boys, asking finally, "Now, *why* do they [girls], why are they acting like adults when we're [boys] still messing around?"

Joseph then went on to answer his own question, maintaining a link between girls' earlier maturity and their longer lives, "It's cos women [.] they grow faster than we do (.) they live longer than we do {I laugh} they, *that* is the truth, like, they're getting more superior than us (.) cos in the past, like, cos we're stronger than them, *we* can seem more superior (.) but as time goes on, we find out that they live longer than us". Again, he voiced his puzzlement at this, "I've been thinking about that, I find it very *strange*, you know, that (.) *why* do girls live longer than boys?" And again attempting to answer his own question, he told me about some episodes of the sci-fi television programme *Sliders*, where there is a nation where traditional gender roles are reversed. Joseph concluded, "I think in a couple of years that will happen [here]".

Joseph's narrative seemed to reflect something of the 'crisis of masculinity' supposedly confronting men at the start of the twenty-first century. He appeared confused by the apparent shifting of roles and anxious about girls' seemingly earlier maturity and men's lack of longevity.

The other narrative used by pupils to oppose Byers' claim was one of individuality, reflecting the discourse of liberal democracy and freedom of choice hegemonic in the West (Walkerdine and Lucey, 1989; Francis, 1999c). For example, Monique (mixed race, year 11) argued that boys can work hard if they want to, and that it is their own (individual) choice. Likewise Charlene (Afro-Caribbean, year 10) maintained that girls can behave in disruptive ways too, and that educational success depends on the individual's attitude to learning. As Triston (Afro-Caribbean, year 10) argued, different ways of behaving are caused by "different person*alities*" rather than gender.

Contradictions in Young People's Talk

Some pupils consistently maintained in their interviews that there is little or no difference in male and female classroom behaviour. A number of these pupils specifically articulated their belief that there are no behavioural differences between men and women, boys and girls. Other pupils argued consistently that there are 'naturally' occurring differences between males and females that permeate classroom behaviour and explain the gender differences therein. However, there were many contradictions in the talk of the majority of pupils about gender, and the most frequently occurring contradiction was a construction the sexes as equal or 'the same' while simultaneously presenting boys and girls as behaving differently, or having different abilities. As reported above, many male and female pupils maintained that 'these days' the sexes are equally able and often that there are no gender differences in terms of behaviour or opportunity. However, many of the same pupils went on to contradict these claims at various points in their interviews, arguing, for example, that girls are more mature than boys, that boys mess around more than girls, or that boys and girls are interested in different things. This point is particularly illustrated by the pupils' response to Stephen Byers' statement on boys' laddish behaviour. As I have reported in other chapters, in response to all the other questions concerning possible gender differences, the majority of pupils replied that such differences between boys and girls no longer exist. Yet in response to this final question, two-thirds of the pupils agreed with Byers that boys' (different) behaviour is affecting their learning.

This apparent contradiction supports my previous finding that people draw on different discourses on gender at different times. Hence, the way in which pupils argued at one moment that girls and boys are the same, or equal, and the next that they are different illustrates the way in which equal opportunities and other equity discourses coexist with discourses of gender difference and anti-equality discourses in the pupils' talk. It also supports findings from my study of primary school children that equal opportunities discourses do not effectively challenge or combat discourses of gender difference (see also the work of Davies, 1989; 1993). This is because discourses of equal opportunity tend to present the genders as worthy of the same opportunities in life *despite* their differences, rather than presenting the genders as basically the same.

Discussion

To summarize the findings, girls' explanations for boys' laddish behaviour tended to be more pejorative than those of boys. Boys more often explained it via 'natural' (inevitable) gender differences, the distractions they face or through the comparative industry of girls, whereas girls were more likely to use social explanations (see Mahony, 1998) and to apportion responsibility to the boys. Just over a quarter of the pupils disagreed with Byers' argument. Of these, many pointed to the academic boys in their classes to demonstrate that not all boys behave 'laddishly', or argued that if they do it does not affect their learning. Others drew on narratives of equal opportunities and individuality to maintain that classroom behaviour depends on the individual rather than on gender.

The analysis of the pupils' explanations for the laddish behaviour of boys in school revealed six different gender discourses underlying the pupils' constructions. These were innate inequality between genders, female superiority, social constructions, active heterosexuality, stereotypically gendered characteristics and behaviour, and women's liberation. Boys drew on the discourse of stereotypically gendered characteristics and behaviour particularly frequently. This sometimes linked to the discourse of innate inequality between genders, as did the discourse of female superiority, which tended to be drawn on by boys and girls for different reasons. However, the discourse of social construction was by far the most commonly used in pupil's explanations. I find this encouraging, because it demonstrates a readiness to explain gender differences in behaviour through social, rather than essentialist or discriminatory explanations and therefore allows for the possibility of change and reconstruction in people's gendered behaviour.

Yet despite this frequent use of the discourse of social construction, the pupils' classroom interaction actually remained strongly gendered, and this seems reflected in their readiness to position boys' behaviour as detrimental to learning. As Volman and Tem Dam (1998) and Holland et al. (1998) have observed, liberal equal opportunities and 'post-feminist' discourses may hide continuing inequality and difference.

Obviously this chapter only examines pupils' responses to Byers' claim concerning boys' behaviour: it does not examine whether boys' laddish behaviour was indeed impeding their learning. Although the classroom observation did suggest that boys tend to be louder and more demanding than girls and use more visible and physical forms of resistance in the classroom, simple, non-longitudinal observational methods cannot reveal conclusively whether such behaviour is hindering boys' learning. Any study that really sought to test this point would have to use multiple methods, observing pupils in the classroom and around the school (plus keeping tabs on their homework practices) and analysing their work and grades. It would also have to be longitudinal. Even in this case, it would be difficult to actually prove that achievement was directly linked to classroom behaviour, owing to the high number of other factors (e.g. home support, inherent ability, teaching methods and rapport) that might make equal, or greater, contributions to the achievements of boys. However, common sense suggests that if boys are being disruptive and distracting the teacher, less actual teaching is going on (as the teacher is forced instead to concentrate on establishing discipline), and therefore less learning is occurring. In this sense, 'laddish' modes of behaviour adopted by some boys may be having a detrimental effect on *all* their classmates' achievements, not just on their own. That two-thirds of the 14- to 16-year-old pupils, including almost two-thirds of the boys, supported Byers' argument over laddish behaviour and learning is startling and lends support to writers such as Salisbury and Jackson (1996) and Pickering (1997), who have made similar points in the past. Boys' disruptive behaviour has long been a feature of school life (Yates, 1997), and to label it 'laddish' is a late 1990s phenomenon. However, if the classroom behaviour and construction of masculinity on the part of some boys is having negative consequences for achievement in school, then it is right that the issue is finally being addressed.

As was observed above, 'laddish' behaviour can sometimes provide light relief in the classroom and consequently be appreciated by other pupils. As the pupils' explanations show, such behaviour in boys is also often constructed as important and desirable in male friendship groups and for attracting girls. This latter point is an important one from a feminist perspective, as it implicates girls (and women) as well as males in the perpetuation of 'laddish' behaviour. Holland et al. (1998) question the view that gender relations are increasingly flexible and negotiable, maintaining instead that despite superficial changes in gender relations 'institutional heterosexuality' continues to position those who do not adhere to strict heterosexual gender norms as deviant. Masculinity and femininity are positioned as relational and oppositional to one another in terms of desired behaviour, and such behaviour is often in turn rewarded with heterosexual attraction. In Chapter 4 I discussed how I, and many teachers (male and female), often found the 'laddish' boys particularly appealing and amusing in the classroom, demonstrating the way in which pupils' constructions of gender generally, and the construction of 'laddish' behaviour as appealing, are shared and reflected in the wider society. The powerful hegemony of the gender dichotomy means that different kinds of behaviour are desired of girls and boys, women and men, and the behaviour of men and women is constructed in different ways (Francis, 1998a). Humour, defiance, strength, bravery, competition and brutality are constructed as being male traits, and they are infused with the desires of both men and women. In this sense, boys' expressions of 'laddism' are an unsurprising reflection of modes of behaviour and values found in the wider society. If we are to disrupt these constructions of gender, we must examine and challenge our own investments of desire in traditional constructions of masculinity.

8 Discussion
Gender, Achievement and Status

The data presented in the previous chapters have built up a picture of gendered interaction in the classroom and pupils' interpretations of this. Their opinions and aspirations have also been analysed by gender. This chapter will examine the consequences of these various constructions with particular reference to power and achievement in the classroom. It begins by summarizing the findings from the study. It then goes on to discuss the implications, with an evaluation of the apparent impact of gender constructions on learning. The various possible causes of boys' comparative underachievement are then discussed, with reference to my findings. Finally, broader issues behind the pupils' gender constructions are analysed, in order to identify strategies for change.

The study findings have shown the consequences of gender constructions for classroom interaction: the pupils' efforts to delineate their gender often led to the taking up of very different sorts of behaviour in the classroom. Many girls used interest in feminine-typed subjects (such as appearance) and behaviour (such as chatting and laughing quietly in groups), to construct their femininity. In turn, many boys used physicality (in terms of dominance of the classroom space, violence, or threatened violence), homophobia and misogyny, shows of heterosexuality and masculine-typed interests to demonstrate their gender allegiance and to construct themselves as masculine. The achievement of constructions of masculinity and femininity potentially held considerable benefits for pupils, sometimes endowing status (and, consequently, power) among peers, but also allowing a construction of oneself as 'normal' and 'not deviant'.

The data presented here, and probably our own memories of school days, remind us how important it can be for secondary school pupils to 'fit in'. Not fitting in (for example being labelled a 'swot', 'sissy', 'slag' or their equivalents) can have devastating consequences for a pupil's school life, with the possibility of being marginalized, ostracized or bullied. It is important to note that the terms I have used ('swot', 'sissy' and 'slag') all boys. Also, boys tend to be noisier than girls, and are therefore disciplined more frequently. This book has confirmed that such loud, physical and sometimes aggressive and/or disruptive behaviour is an integral expression of many boys' constructions of masculinity. I have also argued that although there can be no 'scientific' link made between the classroom behaviour of such boys and the slightly lower GCSE results achieved by boys than by girls, it does seem clear that boys who are spending large proportions of their time in class messing about are impeding their chances of high achievement. Being loud and disruptive hinders the learning of other pupils as well as their own. However, the numerous reports from girls and boys that boys have to appear 'hard' and non-learning oriented in order to impress their friends lends support to the argument made by Salisbury and Jackson that boys' 'macho' (I would say 'laddish') constructions of masculinity are hindering their own learning at school.

I sought to explore the pupils' own opinions concerning gender and learning. The interviews gave a number of pupils the opportunity to voice their concerns that teachers tend to discipline boys particularly frequently or harshly. While noting this finding as a point of concern, and observing that boys were indeed disciplined more frequently than were girls, findings from my observation and from pupils' reports suggested that in the majority of cases boys tend to attract more of the teachers' approbation simply because they are louder and tend to be more openly disruptive in class. However, I did record a small number of occasions when teachers appeared more lenient with girls than with boys. Of course it seems likely that if teachers think of boys as generally more likely to be disruptive than girls, they may expect bad behaviour in boys and perpetuate a self-fulfilling prophecy in disciplining them accordingly.

Questioning the pupils about learning revealed how much perceptions of gender and studentship have changed since the first seminal feminist studies of classroom interaction in the 1980s. Where the male pupil used to personify all that was seen as right and proper in a learner (Walkerdine, 1988), pupils now largely presented an egalitarian view of pupils as equally able at all subjects. Young people's favourite subjects are also now slightly less gender stereotypical than they used to be (although a gendered pattern continues to exist, illuminated in pupils' choice of subject at 'A' level). This shift in pupils' perceptions about gender was particularly highlighted by the fact that, of those pupils who said that one sex or the other tend to make better learners, or be better at various subjects, the majority said that *girls* are better. The issue of masculinity and peer pressure was revisited here, as many of the pupils whom maintained that boys are not as good pupils as girls cited male peer pressure as the explanation for this.

If it is the case that, as some pupils and researchers argue, girls are more learning-focused in the classroom, what could be driving their application? In their discussions of gender issues in the wider society, it became clear that many girls held anxieties regarding the adult workplace, believing it to be a place where sexism and gender discrimination remain rife. I have observed that in terms of the distribution of earnings and power in the labour market, their fears appear justified. Yet girls are now more ambitious concerning their future working lives than ever before. It therefore seems reasonable to argue that many girls feel they must be better than males in order to compete in the labour market on an equal footing. One of the most obvious ways in which they can demonstrate their ability and potential is via qualifications: girls may consequently be particularly highly motivated in school, and this may be reflected in their higher achievement than boys at GCSE level. It was shown that boys as well as girls placed high value on further and higher education as an insurance for success in future employment. However, girls have changed in their prioritization of career (rather than assuming they would simply work until they married and had children, when they would either become secondary breadwinners or quit entirely, see Spender, 1982; Gaskell, 1992). Their changed levels of achievement may to some extent reflect their changed ambitions. And there were a number of suggestions from pupils that some boys either take their future employment for granted or are too busily concerned with living in the present to worry about the future.

Of course, educational achievement did not appear to be so incongruous with the dominant construction of femininity as it did with that of masculinity. Many pupils argued that boys who are academically focused risk being ridiculed by their peers. Here again we can see a shift in girls' constructions of femininity. It was observed in Chapter 5 how research in the 1980s found that adolescent girls did not want to be seen as being clever, as this was seen to make women less, rather than more, desirable. They therefore worried that academic success might intimidate and repel boys and men. Such concerns appeared the last thing on the minds of the girls in my study, many of whom demonstrated an assured, though usually modest, self-confidence in female abilities, and often derided boys' apparent lack of academic application. Yet, the continued construction of femininity as sensible/mature in the classroom, and evidence such as the continued policing of female sexuality shows that secondary school girls' constructions of femininity have not altered extensively in some ways. As Smith (1998) observes, popular constructions of femininity have changed in some respects but remain the same in others. She observes how femininity remains a 'moral condition': women are still expected to be responsible for men, their families and children, and are vilified if they are seen to put their own needs first.

Willis (1977) showed that even in the 1970s, working-class boys saw academic success as incompatible with masculinity. Hence there appears to be continuity in the boys' constructions: academic work and application is associated with femininity. The pupils in my study were largely of working-class origin, and therefore it comes as no surprise that many of their constructions of masculinity bore similarities with those of Willis' 'lads'. Studies by writers such as Mac an Ghaill (1994) have found some evidence that social class impacts on constructions of masculinity and achievement (for example the middle-class 'Real Englishmen' derided the 'Macho Lads' as bestial morons, although continuing to exhibit masculine behaviour by positioning themselves as more capable and knowing than the teachers). Yet Martino's (1999) work in Australia suggests that middle-class boys too are increasingly taking on the macho, anti-school construction of masculinity expressed by Willis' lads.

That there were working-class 'lobes' (academically oriented) boys in Willis' study (and see also Mac an Ghaill, 1994, and others) reminds us of the diversity in boys' positions. As many of the pupils were keen to point out in response to Byers' claims about laddism in Chapter 7, not all boys are disruptive or alienated from academic work. Yet despite this diversity, my classroom observation showed that generally boys were louder and more disruptive than girls in the classroom: many girls and boys supported Byers' claim that such 'laddish' behaviour is impeding boys' achievement at school. Moreover, the explanations of the majority of these pupils supported the arguments made by Salisbury and Jackson (1996) and Pickering (1997) that it is boys' collective constructions of masculinity, and the peer pressure of gender role maintenance, that causes this behaviour.

With these findings in mind, the next section turns again to the debate on boys' achievement, comparing the various explanations for boys' comparative underachievement with my findings. However, before I begin discussing this issue, I want to reiterate the point that boys as a whole are not 'underachieving'. As was observed in Chapter 1, the GCSE results of boys are actually improving year on year, and in many subjects their outperformance by girls is actually very slight. Other structural differences, such as social class, actually have a greater impact on achievement than does gender. However, it is certainly the case that boys are lagging behind girls at language subjects in a way which should not be seen as acceptable, and therefore the issue of gender and achievement does merit attention.

The Causes of Boys' Underachievement

There are broadly two explanations for boys' failure to match girls in terms of achievement at GCSE level. The first emanates from the 'poor boys' discourse identified by Epstein et al. (1998), which argues that boys are now disadvantaged in schools. In this discourse, girls' improvements are often presented as having been at the expense of boys. Cohen (1998) has shown how low educational achievement among boys is seen as the result of external faults, such as the teacher, school, or method of learning or assessment. So suggested remedies to improve boys' educational achievement emanating from the 'poor boys' camp tend to be based on a supposition that boys' comparative underachievement results from a failure to make education sufficiently appealing to boys. Hence many educational initiatives include ideas such as providing more non-fictional reading material, using whole-class teaching methods and capturing boys' attention by reference to traditionally male pastimes (see, for example, Clark, 1998; Department of Education and Employment, 1998b; Qualification and Curriculum Authority, 1998).

The other explanation for boys' failure to match girls in terms of their achievement blames schoolboy culture, behaviour or constructions of masculinity. This viewpoint can be illustrated by the speech made by Minister Stephen Byers concerning boys' laddish behaviour, discussed in the previous chapter, and by researchers such as Younger and Warrington (1996), Salisbury and Jackson (1996) and Younger et al. (1999), who argue that boys' 'macho values' or particular constructions of masculinity are harming boys' chances of educational success by positioning such success as 'non-macho'. Hence in this view, if boys are seen to be taking schoolwork, study and educational achievement seriously, they are at risk of being constructed as non-masculine and consequently being ridiculed or marginalized by their peers.

So, which of these viewpoints presents the more accurate picture? A large body of feminist research suggests that rather than the curriculum and learning materials being too 'girl-centred' (as maintained by the 'poor boys' camp), the school curriculum has always reflected and favoured the interests of boys at the expense of girls, and a far greater proportion of teacher time and attention is spent on boys than on girls (Spender, 1982; Stanworth, 1981; Paechter, 1998). Feminist researchers used this evidence in the early 1980s to explain *girls'* lack of educational achievement compared with boys. Yet, as I observed in the first chapter, almost two decades on, research shows that girl's educational achievement has improved *despite* the continuing male dominance of classroom interaction, curriculum content and greater demands on teacher time (Skelton, 1997; Howe, 1997; Francis, 1998a). Hence various researchers have queried the implication in the 'poor boys' perspective that girls' increasing educational success has been at the expense of boys.

Some feminist researchers have argued that girls' improved achievement at GCSE level may be the result of the removal of previous barriers to their attainment and changed expectations on the part of girls (Francis, 1998a; Epstein et al., 1998). The findings presented in this book provide evidence to support this argument, showing that girls are now far more ambitious concerning their careers than was the case in the past. Yet when asked whether gender impacts on one's life, many girls voiced their anxiety that sexism and discrimination still permeate various facets of the labour market. As was noted above, if girls seek careers, but are sceptical about the extent of equal opportunities in the workplace, this awareness of continuing discrimination may well act as a spur to educational achievement, as qualifications are seen as an obvious way by which to demonstrate one's intellect and potential.

Hence the assumption that girls are outperforming boys because boys' needs have been marginalized in the classroom would seem a misguided one. But what of the view that boys' constructions of masculinity are at odds with educational achievement? The fact that many boys are extremely successful at GCSE level, and the continuing success of boys at 'A' and degree level, shows that this cannot be true of all boys. As I noted in my classroom observation and as several of the pupils pointed out in their interviews, many boys are extremely academically focused.[1] Boys construct masculinity in different ways, and some may not attempt to construct themselves as particularly masculine at all (either because they do not wish to, or because they do not have the necessary resources). For *some* boys a construction of masculinity may involve a rejection of school values, whereas for others they may use aspects of those very values (for instance a competitive approach to learning and achievement) to construct their masculinity. As was shown by the behaviour of Saul and Wesley in Chapter 4, boys particularly well-resourced and successful in their constructions of masculinity may be able to incorporate a number of different, sometimes apparently feminine, facets without challenge to their masculine constructions.

However, it has been shown in previous chapters that a construction of masculinity as 'laddish' appears the most accepted one among 14- to 16-year-old pupils, certainly in the largely working-class schools in which I conducted the research. A laddish persona appears able to incorporate more of the traits that are traditionally seen and valued as masculine than can other constructions; for example, interest in masculine-typed activities such as football, the objectification of and sexual activity with females, an irreverent and rebellious attitude to authority, physical strength, boisterousness, bravery, daring, camaraderie and 'having a laugh'. As Skelton (1999) and Martino (1999) observe, in this schema it becomes far more important to be seen as able at sports than at academic work. Indeed, two traits required of pupils in the classroom and in relation to schoolwork, obedience and diligence, are in direct opposition to a laddish construction of masculinity (and, arguably, to constructions of masculinity generally). Values such as irreverence, daring and 'having a laugh' mean that in the classroom disruption and resistance are integral facets of the laddish construction. In this sense, a construction of laddish masculinity does have implications for learning, particularly in areas of schoolwork that require concentration and diligence. The pupils' interview responses concerning the notion of 'laddish behaviour' broadly supported this interpretation. The majority argued that the term 'laddish' is representative of some or all boys in the classroom, and that such behaviour has a negative effect on their learning. Of those that speculated about the causes of laddish behaviour, most pupils' arguments evoked the notion of social constructions of masculinity, claiming that boys behave in such ways in order to portray themselves as 'hard' and/or to impress their friends.

So boys that construct themselves as 'lads' may be impeding learning and, consequently, achievement. It is important to remember, however, that the learning they are impeding is not just their own: the behaviour of loud and disruptive boys also distracts their male and female classmates. Further, the time that the teacher spends disciplining such boys detracts from the time devoted to teaching the class. Hence it could be said that such behaviour disadvantages *all* pupils, although obviously it is likely to have a particular effect on these boys' own progress.

Therefore, in terms of achievement, this book has shown two things. It has shown that a particular construction of masculinity (the laddish one) can have negative consequences for learning. And it has shown that girls have more motivation to achieve than used to be the case, concerned as they are to pursue careers in what they often see as a male-dominated and gender discriminatory workplace.

Continuity and Change in Constructions of Gender

So girls' constructions of the female role have altered over the past two decades, and this is having a positive effect on their achievement. But what of boys? The findings in this book show that their constructions of masculinity have largely remained the same.

Many writers have suggested the contrary view that boys' constructions have changed dramatically (particularly due to the 'crisis of masculinity'). Yet there appears little evidence for such claims. Arnot et al. (1999) maintain that boys' concepts of masculinity have been affected by the economic restructuring of the 1980s, and that consequently boys have been "compelled to find new ways of celebrating manhood" (p. 142). Yet, conversely, my findings from largely working-class secondary schools record little change

Having said all this, if girls have changed their constructions of femininity (for example to include the possibility of academic success and the wish for a career), why is it that boys' constructions of masculinity remain largely unchanged? As was famously pointed out by the *Panorama* programme 'The Future is Female', communications and literacy skills are increasingly necessary in the workplace, because of the expansion of the service sector. Moreover, as women enter the labour market in growing numbers, one might have assumed that many men would have jumped at the opportunity to take on more involvement with childcare. As women moved into traditionally male spheres, so men might have advanced into traditionally female roles and areas of work. Certainly, families might be more effective with a more gender equitable split in responsibilities between partners. It should be acknowledged that there has been some shift in attitudes among men and boys concerning roles appropriate for men and women (Francis, 1998a; Redman, 1998; Arnot et al., 1999). Yet generally studies consistently find boys' views on gender-appropriate roles to be more conservative than those of girls.[2]

Boys' constructions of desirable forms of masculinity remain predominantly unchanged because these reflect those of the broader society, in which constructions of desirable masculinity are also largely unchanged (as I shall discuss below). There seem to be two possible reasons why constructions of masculinity have remained largely constant despite the shift in girls' and women's constructions to accommodate a move into traditionally masculine areas. The first is that to alter constructions to accommodate, for instance, more caring and communicative behaviour might risk the male construction of self-sufficiency, self-confidence and strength/aggression, which currently allow them acceptance to the masculine 'club' and elevation over women. In other words, to become more 'feminine' would be to give up power. This is crudely put: it is recognized that not all men automatically have power over women. Foucault's work[3] has shown us that power is not a possession, but rather that power relationships are constantly shifting and changing in interaction. Yet generally in school and the wider society, men monopolize the positions of power, and male values are taken as the benchmark of normality.

The second possibility is that, because masculinity is constructed in relation to and opposition to femininity, men seek to delineate their masculinity by adamantly perpetuating traditional constructions. This raises the concept of a 'flight from femininity'. The idea being that, rather as the British Conservative Party is currently moving to the right as New Labour encroaches the middle ground of political ideology, so boys are becoming increasingly laddish in their efforts to construct themselves as non-feminine as girls move into areas traditionally seen as masculine. As was observed earlier, some researchers have argued that laddish constructions of masculinity tend to be taken up particularly by working-class boys. As the majority of pupils at the schools in which I conducted research were working class, my findings are unable to shed much light on this theory. Yet Martino's (1999) study of Australian boys shows how, in their efforts to construct girls and male 'squids' (swots) as 'other', many middle-class 'cool' boys adopted what Martino calls 'protest masculinity', behaving in laddish ways to demonstrate their opposition to academic orientation. Likewise, in Britain, Power et al. (1998) have shown that some middle-class boys appear to be increasingly focusing on sport in opposition to a schoolwork ethos. If girls' constructions of gender are becoming more diverse, it is possible that boys are being increasingly forced to adopt hyper-masculine constructions in order to depict their difference from girls. This would bring us back to the question of why it might appear so important to boys to maintain this difference, arguably answered by my former point that boys (and men) seek to preserve their dominance.

Further, laddish attitudes are still portrayed as desirable in the wider society. In previous chapters I have argued that the majority of the attributes of the laddish boys are highly valued as masculine traits, and that as a consequence many other boys, girls and adults find 'laddish' boys particularly appealing. Yet these laddish attitudes have been shown to potentially impede achievement at secondary school. So do we want boys to change?

Which Way for Masculinity?

It is ironic that in a climate of concern over boys' achievement levels, the findings from this study suggest that many teachers (and other adults such as myself) are amused by the antics of class clowns and often find that some of the most successfully masculine boys are their most appealing pupils. Yet this has probably always been the case. Teachers are only human after all, and, although it is a teacher's job to avoid favouring some pupils at the expense of others, it is inevitable that their values will largely reflect those dominant in society when it comes to deciding what is attractive or appealing. In Western societies, characteristics such as risk, wit, resistance, strength, virility, defiance, sporting prowess, humour and competitiveness are highly prized in males. The majority of male hero characters in films, TV, comics and other facets of popular culture embody these traits, illuminating the point that the most desirable men are 'properly' masculine. Traditionally, the male hero has been responsible, decisive and in control: a 'real man'. Yet with the emergence of 'new laddism' in the 1990s, there appears to have sprouted a cult of juvenility in constructions of masculinity. In this construction, men cling to their 'boyishness', elevating the characteristics of irresponsibility, irreverence and silly, mischievous fun. (This position can be illustrated by television programmes such as *Men Behaving Badly*, *Fantasy Football* and *They Think It's All Over*, magazines such as *Loaded*, and novels by writers such as Nick Hornby, Mike Gayle and David Baddiel.) This of course shows how boys' 'silly' laddish constructions can sit even more easily with constructions of masculinity dominant in the wider society than was the case in the past.

Yet it also shows how constructions of masculinity can and do shift. Although boys' dominant constructions of masculinity in the secondary school classroom show little alteration, boys' views of gender roles in the wider society have been found to show some signs of change. And again, although there is strong evidence of continuity here too, dominant constructions of masculinity in popular culture often appear more complex than has been the case in the past. It now often appears insufficient for heroes simply to be macho: the 'ideal man' must also possess a sense of irony and be able to laugh at himself (and others). Although remaining small compared with the female market, the growth in sales of designer menswear, perfumery and cosmetic products suggests that men are taking more care of their appearance than they used to do. (Albeit, as Salisbury and Jackson (1996) note, the naming, packaging and marketing of such products often emphasize the active, masculine virility of the product and its user, hence protecting male purchasers from accusations of being too feminine.) This new focus on appearance can conversely reflect a desire to appear *more* masculine: some men are seeking to make their bodies fit more easily into the heterosexual norm of masculine desirability. Bodybuilding provides a good example here. Yet this new preoccupation with appearance on the part of some men is often derided by others, because it is a traditionally *feminine* characteristic, even when used in an endeavour to appear more masculine.

Having concluded that a culture of laddish masculinity remains largely unchanged in schools, it is important we do not simply sit back and accept this. Arnot et al. (1999) point out that the equal opportunities programmes of the 1980s were exclusively geared towards girls: programmes were devised to encourage girls at subjects such as maths and science, and to assert themselves at school. Yet no real attempt was made by feminists or policy makers to encourage boys in the arts or humanities, or to address forms of masculinity in the classroom. Arnot et al. argue convincingly that this failure to address boys' masculine constructions has had negative repercussions for boys. Hence it is important that this situation is addressed now. The laddish masculine culture is potentially damaging to non-laddish boys, who are often subject to ridicule, abuse and physical bullying by more laddish boys, and to girls, who are marginalized by laddish boys' dominance of the classroom, and who may also be the victims of their sexism and misogyny. It is also damaging to the laddish boys themselves. Speaking on BBC News (18 October 1999) a spokesman for The Samaritans blamed 'boys' culture of laddism' for the high incidence of suicide among young men. He argued that their laddish personas prevent them from expressing their feelings, reporting that in response to The Samaritan's survey, two-thirds of boys said they have no-one they can talk to about intimate problems. The theme of desire for intimacy and support was echoed in my study by the boys' often wistful talk about girls' friendships compared with their own. As I observed when watching the reactions of pupils to Ms N's baby, boys are no less warm or caring than girls; it is simply less acceptable for them to express these feelings.

As I argued above, in today's economic climate it is increasingly important that boys are encouraged to develop their communication skills. Boys' laddish constructions are impeding their development of such skills, hence potentially disadvantaging them in the labour market. This lack of communication skills also hinders boys' educational achievement at English and languages, besides jeopardizing their educational achievement generally due to the laddish construction's positioning of school-based learning as feminine. Hence the dominant construction of masculinity disadvantages boys and girls in the classroom and can also damage the future prospects of boys. We need to encourage boys to understand the consequences of their behaviour and to expand their constructions and outlooks. The next chapter explores the means by which this might be achieved.

9 Teaching Strategies for the Future

Teachers confronting underachievement among their pupils often do not have time to pore over tomes about gender theory, nor do they have time to devise their own ways in which to apply such theory to their classroom practice. Rather, they want practical strategies and suggestions with which to combat underachievement. Since 1995 a large body of literature has sprung up aiming to supply this demand. This chapter will argue, however, that many of the tips and strategies offered in such books can only make a superficial difference to the issue of boys' underperformance, as they do not address one of the main underlying causes of boys' lesser educational success: the perpetuation of a laddish gender culture among school boys. The previous chapter showed why it is so important that we attempt to challenge this culture, and indeed I argue the importance of encouraging diverse subject positions for girls and boys. Yet as this chapter will illustrate, this will be far more difficult and challenging than introducing many of the ideas suggested in the dominant literature on boys' underachievement.

Problems Caused by a Simply Pragmatic Approach

This section seeks to demonstrate why it is imperative that suggestions for combating underachievement in schools are based on sound research and a clear understanding of gender issues. The intention is not to belittle the general body of work in this area; indeed, it will be argued that many of the useful strategies forwarded in this work can be combined with a broader strategy for addressing constructions of gender polarity. However, it is important to realize that some 'intuitive' strategies and an inconsistent approach to the issue of gender and achievement can be counterproductive. They can actually strengthen the oppositional gender cultures that I and others have argued contribute to boys' underperformance at GCSE level compared with girls.

An example can be provided by the strategies used to encourage boys to feel more interested in school and learning via the use of sport. The Department for Education and Employment is currently piloting homework clubs located in football clubs (Department of Education and Employment, 1998b). When this initiative was announced, ministers maintained that girls too might benefit from these clubs, but were unabashed in their acknowledgement that the initiative was targeted at boys. Connolly (1998) describes how, at a primary school in which he conducted research, a headteacher was specifically attempting to regain apparently alienated boys' enthusiasm for school by encouraging competitive sport and demonstrating his own passion for sport with the boys. Similarly, in his foreword to Bleach's book, Tim Brighouse (1998) suggests that a headteacher's regular questioning of boys about sport encouraged their achievement in his school.

However, findings in this book, and by Skelton (1999; 2000), Connolly (1998), Martino (1999) and Pattman et al. (1999) have shown how sport, particularly football, plays an important part in boys' construction of laddish masculinity. Indeed, boys in this study actually blamed football specifically as one of the main distractions that impede their educational achievement. If a passion for football and other forms of competitive sport help boys to forge the laddish construction of masculinity that can impede their learning, it seems an odd educational policy to deliberately encourage them in this. Further, little thought appears to have been given in such initiatives to the boys (and girls) who do not like, or are not good at, sport. Connolly (1998) found that football games in particular seemed to encourage expressions of racism and bullying among boys, with a masculine hierarchy being clearly delineated around those who were good at football and those boys who were not skilled at, or disliked, football. Connolly also suggests that the headteacher's elevation of boys skilled at sports (via his interest in them expressed by banter, chats about sport and kickabouts with them in the playground, along with their regular celebration for their sporting achievements in assemblies) marginalized other boys and girls and appeared to disproportionately reward boys who were also sometimes the most disruptive in the classroom. Skelton (2000) explained how male teachers' support of and collaboration with a macho culture based around football had the effect of marginalizing girls and seemed to heighten the importance of sporting ability in a successful construction of masculinity, which can only have served to make the position of non-sporting boys more insecure.

Another example of a strategy for combating underachievement that actually supports the construction of gender polarity among pupils is that of separate reading boxes for girls and boys. Obviously literacy, English and languages are the areas in which boys' underachievement is most marked, and it has been observed in many studies that boys appear to read less than do girls. Some writers have suggested that this is because boys see reading

emphasize the importance of clear and firm deadlines, and of short-term target setting, with regular individual meetings with pupils in order to set these targets. Pickering argues that short-term target setting is an effective strategy for raising and monitoring boys' achievement. And MacDonald et al. (1999) observe the importance of early identification, with speedy intervention, of those pupils at risk of failing.

A further point of consensus in the considered work exploring gender and achievement is that it is useful to consult pupils themselves about gender issues and curriculum development. Pupils will appreciate their opinions being taken into consideration, and their views can also be helpful and revealing (Penny, 1998). Pickering (1997) recommends that teachers do not talk *about* boys but rather talk with them. His own work illustrates how difficult it can be to avoid talking about 'the boys' and 'the girls' when discussing gender and underachievement, as his recommendations for change include talking about the underachievement issue with boys and analysing boys' behaviour and attitudes with colleagues. However, his intention to avoid problematizing 'the boys' is an important one, particularly bearing in mind the findings that boys feel victimized by teachers. Consulting pupils about their views of school and the subjects and activities they engage in has been found illuminating by a number of writers (e.g. Pickering, 1997; Penny, 1998). However, if embarking on broad-scale consultation, particularly in the form of questionnaires, it is important to bear in mind that gender constructions motivate the pupils' answers. Therefore, it may, for example, appear more acceptable to girls to respond that they enjoy school and school-based activity than it does for boys, even if boys actually gain as much pleasure from school as girls do. Such responses can be useful for illuminating trends in pupils' views; yet they should not necessarily be interpreted as reflecting a 'real' picture.

Linked with the notion of consultation with pupils is Bleach's (1998b) suggestion that assessment of pupils' work and progress should allow for some pupil self-evaluation and discussion. Such processes can help pupils to understand more closely the various factors considered in assessment and hence more effectively to assess their own work as they produce it (besides feeling empowered by the knowledge that the teacher takes them seriously). It is important that such increased self-assessment is performed in conjunction with teacher assessment and explanation, however, as evidence shows that boys tend to be overconfident concerning their abilities, whereas girls undersell themselves (Stanworth, 1981; Bleach, 1998a). (This reinforces Connolly's (1998) concern that an overfocus on praising boys marginalizes girls: girls need just as much encouragement.) Pickering (1997) and MacDonald et al. (1999) remind us of the importance of being positive and encouraging pupils in general, in order to increase their self-esteem and enthusiasm for the work. They argue that pupils' improved behaviour, work and/or effort should be immediately rewarded.

Many writers have also stressed the importance of parental involvement in supporting the school's efforts to improve achievement (e.g. Frater, 1998; MacDonald et al., 1999). Because the biggest gaps between boys' and girls' achievement are in the areas of English and languages, much of the literature on gender and achievement especially focuses on literacy. Parental support is particularly stressed here; for example, Frater (1998) argues that parents should be told to listen to their children reading at home. Given the concern that boys tend to see reading as a feminine activity, and Reay's (1998) finding that the vast majority of learning support at home is carried out by mothers, perhaps fathers should be particularly encouraged to read with boys. Other strategies for improving literacy that appear to hold some unanimity across the literature are target setting for reading and literacy skills, a focus on literacy across the curriculum, and ensuring that the criteria for assessment of coursework is made explicit. Penny (1998) and Pickering (1997) both recommend the use of writing frames in English to help pupils structure their writing. Penny maintains that, more than this, writing frames should include linguistic devices to hold the text together, as boys particularly tend to lack resources in this area.

The strategies reported here have largely been tested by a number of authors and are based on research and literature reviews. They may, therefore, provide useful tools and approaches for teachers aiming to raise achievement in their classrooms, particularly when coupled with a broader focus on challenging established gender constructions.

Teachers' Attitudes to Boys and Girls

A further factor that might affect boys' achievement and attitudes to school are the responses of teachers to them. My own research and findings by Younger and Warrington (1996); Pickering (1997), Younger et al. (1999) show that many boys feel, rightly or wrongly, that they are 'picked on' by teachers, whereas girls escape punishment for similar offences. Many girls actually support this interpretation. I have noted in the last chapter that I found only very limited evidence of such practices; yet it seems important that teachers be made aware of boys' concerns. If boys are discriminated against in terms of disciplinary practices, it increases the likelihood of their becoming alienated from school. However, teachers obviously have to tread an extremely difficult path regarding gender and discipline; my findings suggest that for the most part, boys are told off more than girls because they tend to be louder, more overtly disruptive and to draw attention to themselves more than do the majority of girls. The case may sometimes arise when a group of boys and a group of girls are talking among themselves while a teacher attempts to address the class: the teacher may be driven to discipline the boys while ignoring the girls because the boys are making more noise, thus causing more of a distraction. Or perhaps the teacher may not even notice that the girls are talking. Moreover, should teachers, in their anxiety not to alienate boys, become more lenient with them, they risk the possibility of discriminating against girls, and indeed of a breakdown of discipline in the classroom.

The other side of this coin is the amount of teacher time devoted to boys, often at the expense of girls. My findings show that teachers continue to spend, on average, more time engaging with boys in the class. This is partly because the teacher spends more time disciplining boys, but boys also tend to ask more questions and shout out more answers than do girls. (Younger et al. (1999) found that, although boys ask more questions than do girls, these are often incidental. Girls ask questions less frequently, but when they do they seem to use the teacher as a resource more effectively, as their questions tend to be more constructive. Salisbury and Jackson (1996) argue that boys are scared to ask meaningful questions for fear of seeming foolish before their male peers.) There was also the issue of the different approaches taken by some teachers to boys and girls: a number of teachers appeared to take a particularly abrasive, 'roustabout' attitude with boys, which can only serve to compound the construction of gender difference in the classroom and to endorse the laddish construction of masculinity. Skelton (2000) has pointed out that such behaviour is sometimes used by male teachers to construct their own masculinity in the classroom.

This subtle endorsement of boys' laddish construction of masculinity is not, however, limited to male teachers. It has been discussed how I and a number of other teachers derived amusement from the antics of some of these boys. Further, that I and some of the teachers seemed to find these very boys particularly appealing. Of course, these were largely the boys that were able to play up the charmingly roguish, rather than overtly aggressive, aspects of the laddish construction. However, the suggestion that we actually collaborate in the perpetuation of boys' constructions, either by actively collaborating with their behaviour in class, or more passively rewarding them with our admiration, is a point of concern if we believe that these constructions of masculinity are impeding their academic application.

Regarding the issues of gender, discipline and teacher time, it was suggested in Chapter 4 that teachers reflect on their disciplinary practices in order to check that they are not inequitable. Younger et al. (1999) found teachers to be very realistic and open concerning their treatment of pupils according to gender: the majority of teachers sought to be fair and were aware of many gender issues, yet also recognized that in reality gender might impact on their interaction with pupils. It was suggested in Chapter 4 that teachers might consider the frequency with which they discipline girls and boys and whether the proportions actually reflect pupil behaviour. Further, that teachers might attempt to observe, or persuade a colleague to observe for them, how much time is spent interacting with boys and girls during lessons. Concerning the even more complex and uncomfortable possibility that we are sometimes complicit in perpetuating laddish classroom behaviour, both teachers and researchers like myself must reflect on our interaction with boys and girls in the classroom. Are we rewarding particular types of behaviour? Do we actually see academically oriented pupils as boring or conformist, and, if so, how can we berate less academically oriented boys for their underachievement?

As I have maintained above, it is surely important that schools encourage *all* pupils to speculate and question, to ably consider and discuss different ideas and to take a real interest in their learning. Schools should also provide pupils with the skills necessary to cope in society and with the ability to develop their own learning paths. The construction of gender polarity taken up by pupils tends to position 'attitude' (questioning, challenging, 'having a laugh') as masculine and in opposition to academic application (diligence, pleasure in learning), which is constructed as feminine. My point is that there is no reason why 'attitude' and academic application should be seen as incompatible. A questioning, challenging attitude can greatly enhance a passion for and understanding of a subject. Yet in terms of achievement and understanding, attitude is of little use without application and a good command of the skills necessary to produce schoolwork. We should endeavour to encourage both 'attitude' and application in all our pupils, irrespective of their gender, and this may be the key to improving achievement. Yet in order to do so we will need to deconstruct the oppositional construction that locates attitude in the male, and application in the female, in the classroom.

What can be done to Address and Change Dominant Gender Constructions?

We need then, to challenge the construction of gender opposition that allocates different types of behaviour to either the masculine or the feminine, subsequently encouraging pupils to avoid different types of behaviour according to their gender. It is easy to see that this is a far more difficult and complex challenge than, say, increasing short-term target setting in classroom practice. However, the evidence built up in this book, supported by the findings of other writers, suggests that it is the only way to tackle the root causes of difference in achievement according to gender. After all, the majority of research-based literature investigating pupils' attitudes and their relation to boys' underachievement shows that boys position school-based learning as a feminine activity. And further, that it is boys themselves that police and maintain this construction among the male peer group, rejecting boys who appear too learning oriented (Younger and Warrington, 1996; Pickering, 1997; Martino, 1999).

So how to approach this difficult task? Although the notion of challenging and breaking down the gender dichotomy is not a new one, there has been very little work suggesting practical ways in which to go about this. Indeed, detailed investigations to evaluate which strategies and materials are effective in deconstructing oppositional constructions of gender in schools are urgently needed and are recommended as an area of further research.

However, there have been a small number of attempts to engage with this notion in classroom practice. Bronwyn Davies (1993) concluded that the 'gender duality', which locks girls and boys into different sets of behaviour and consequently unequal power relations in the classroom, could be combated by teaching children about post-structuralist theory. She argued that only post-structuralist discourse analysis can reveal the ways in which we are positioned in the gender discourses that allocate various traits and modes of behaviour to one gender or the other. Hence, it is only by understanding and using discourse analysis that children (and adults) can set about deconstructing the gender discourses that restrict their lives. I have discussed Davies' endeavours to teach children post-structuralist discourse analysis elsewhere (Francis, 1998a). While praising her efforts to provide children with the resources with which to challenge the gender dichotomy, and noting her success in getting children to think critically about gender constructions, I suggested that the post-structuralist aspect of this work was less significant than was her feminist stance. Davies herself admitted that primary school children had difficulty understanding some of the key concepts of post-structuralism (hardly surprising, for they continue to baffle many academics!). Further, I have pointed out that teaching young people post-structuralist theory does not necessarily mean that they will wish to deconstruct the gender dichotomy in which we all have much of our sense of identity invested. However, the work of Davies (1993) and other feminist or pro-feminist educationalists (e.g. Salisbury and Jackson, 1996; Wing, 1997; Yeoman, 1999) demonstrates the possibility of getting young people to think critically about constructions of gender in the classroom and the wider society. Indeed, the findings of these researchers suggests room for cautious optimism, because the work of many of the pupils they taught showed signs of new ways of thinking about gender.

I have also argued that in devising methods for addressing the gender dichotomy with pupils, it is imperative that we bear in mind the importance of these traditional gender discourses for pupils and our own senses of identity (Francis, 1998a). The previous chapter discussed how a successful construction of gender can ensure that a pupil will be seen as 'normal' by their peers. That successful gender constructions rest on an assumption of behavioural polarity between boys and girls means that pupils who adopt non-traditional positions potentially disrupt the security of the gender constructions of others around them. It is this danger that motivates 'gender role maintenance', as pupils police the gender constructions of others through peer acceptance or rejection (Davies, 1989). The work of Davies (1989; 1993) and myself (1998a) has illustrated the danger and consequences of being relegated to the 'gender margins' and ridiculed or ostracized by peers if young people take up non-traditional constructions. That we find particular expressions of masculinity in boys and femininity in girls 'natural' or appealing also points to our own immersion in dominant gender discourses. Hence we can see the strength of the forces that we attempt to challenge in deconstructing gender constructions and the risks involved for pupils in engaging with such ideas. Pupils will need more than a few token gestures to set them thinking about these issues seriously and reflecting on their own behaviour.

For this reason, it is imperative that pupils are not given the impression that deconstructing current gender constructions is about simple role reversal (something Davies, 1993, found that children have a tendency to assume). It should be stressed that deconstruction allows both genders the freedom to experiment with more positions than is currently the case, without penalty. It is also important that any strategies adopted go beyond simple equal opportunities approaches. In Chapter 7 I explained Davies' (1989; 1993) argument that equal opportunities discourse presents the genders as different, but endowed them with the right to engage in pursuits traditionally performed by the opposite sex if they so desire. In this sense, equal opportunities discourse supports, rather than challenges, the construction of gender polarity on which sexist and discriminatory discourses are based. This argument was supported by findings from my research with primary school children (Francis, 1998a). I found that the only discourse with potential for deconstructing the gender dichotomy was that of innate equality between the sexes. Even this discourse, which presents the genders as the same, did not always preclude the use of gender discriminatory discourses and other discursive contradiction in children's talk. However, a number of children did use this discourse to argue consistently in their interviews that people are the same irrespective of their gender.

Ideas for Teaching Practice

Talks and Debates on Constructions of Gender

Any strategies for deconstructing constructions of gender polarity in the classroom will involve talking with pupils. Discussion of gender issues in the classroom and wider society is not incompatible with the National Curriculum: it can be incorporated into many different subjects as part of the citizenship theme. There are many ways in which a discussion or study of gender constructions can be structured. Yeoman (1999) found that exposure of pupils to 'disruptive', non-traditional texts and critical reading activities can help to challenge dominant gender discourses and to open up alternatives. I have suggested anti-sexist stories as a good starting point in the primary school, with an ensuing discussion of any differences children could spot between these and more traditional stories leading to a fuller debate about gender roles generally. After discussing constructions in the context of a story that actively challenges traditional gender positions, more traditional stories (in children's books or other media such as TV programmes) can be explored and interrogated. It would be possible to use similar techniques in the secondary school.

Wing (1997) suggests that in adopting this method, the critical factors for success are a text that pupils can identify with and an opportunity to express their own opinions (and to listen to those of others) under the teacher's supervision. Texts in which females and males are presented in non-traditional ways could be juxtaposed with more traditional ones and discussed by the class. Non-traditional materials might include female-centred films or cartoons (or those with strong female roles). Or in English classes, women-centred books portraying powerful women. Traditional materials might include stereotypical portrayals of women as sex objects or victims in tabloid newspapers, macho heroes and storylines in action films or boys' comics, or in English classes, books such as Austen's Jane Eyre, which portray traditional gender roles (the study of such texts can provide valuable reading practice, as Epstein, 1993, points out). The teacher can ask the class to work in groups to identify the ways in which men and women are presented in these texts and to identify the differences between the contrasting texts. Here big sheets of paper can be provided and a 'brain-storming' approach encouraged, so that pupils can list the gender differences and feed back their observations to the class.

A follow-on exercise in English classes might be to give pupils the task of writing new stories, or different endings to traditional texts, that disrupt traditional gender roles. In terms of the continuation of the classroom discussion, teachers might ask pupils how (if at all) expectations of gendered behaviour have changed in recent times, and how acceptable it is for men and women to express the various traits that the pupils have allocated to the opposite sex. These ideas can be fully debated. After this discussion of the traditional ways in which women and men are expected to behave, and the attributes traditionally admired in men and women, the next stage would be to turn the discussion to gender constructions in school. Pupils could be asked whether the attributes that they had allocated as masculine or feminine tend to be expressed by pupils in school, and whether or not there are any other general differences in behaviour according to gender. It is important that this debate is not allowed to become personal: the teacher should firmly make it clear that individuals should not be mentioned in such discussion. If the teacher wishes to provide prompts with which to frame this debate, findings such as those presented in this book on gendered classroom behaviour can be reported.

Teachers may find it useful to bring gender and achievement into the debate, explaining how secondary school girls have gone from comparative underachievement 20 years ago to equalling or outperforming boys in the majority of subjects and asking pupils for their explanations of this phenomenon. If boys' anti-school attitudes are mentioned, the teacher can build on such comments, relating them back to the lists of traits identified as masculine and asking the pupils to reflect on whether or not the dominant construction of masculinity can incorporate an enthusiasm for learning. If the issue of boys' (laddish) attitudes is not raised by the pupils themselves, the teacher might introduce the link between the gender constructions that had been discussed and the issue of achievement. Again, findings from this book, or Byers' statement about boys' laddish behaviour impeding their learning, might be used to provoke debate. However, it is important that one particular gender does not become unduly problematized, or that the debate be allowed to deteriorate into a 'boys versus girls' one. The question of the harsher disciplining of boys by teachers might be raised for discussion to balance any focus on their comparative underachievement. And the use of mixed-sex small-group work, with groups then feeding back their ideas to the class, will help to diffuse the potential for 'battle of the sexes' scenarios in the classroom.

The work by Wing (1997) and Yeoman (1999) shows that the role of the teacher is crucial in making these methods effective. Some might question whether attempts to challenge pupils' gender constructions are desirable or justifiable, suggesting as it does a moral imposition by the teacher. As a feminist I believe that such efforts are justified in their pursuit of equity and will benefit both girls and boys by potentially allowing them to take up more flexible subject positions, thus freeing them from some of the more repressive aspects of traditional gender positions. Moreover, this book has also shown that such an approach may have a beneficial impact on boys' educational achievement.

In attempting to challenge dominant gender constructions, a neutral, 'objective' stance by the teacher will be inadequate. In her work on anti-racist strategies in the classroom, Epstein (1993) has shown that if a teacher allows racist or sexist comments to go unchallenged in discussion it can have the effect of legitimizing these remarks. She also maintains that pupils will see a teacher's supposed neutrality as a fallacy. She agrees that discussion ought to be open, and that particular comments should not be banned or ridiculed (it is important that they are brought into the open). However, sexist, homophobic or racist comments must be seriously discussed and questioned and, where possible, evidence provided to challenge reactionary assumptions. Epstein suggests an approach whereby the teacher explains her/his standpoint at the beginning of the discussion, encouraging pupils to share their views and explaining that there are no right or wrong answers. As I have argued, pupils have much invested in the maintenance of gender difference, and it will therefore require a pro-equity approach to persuade them to begin to question their assumptions. As I have noted elsewhere (Francis, 1998a), it is imperative that pupils are provided with an alternative discourse (gender equity) with which to replace the construction of gender polarity.

Single-sex Workshops

I have suggested that if gender constructions are addressed in whole-class sessions at co-ed schools, mixed-sex, small-group work on particular tasks may be effective in keeping the lesson focused and in diffusing possible counterproductive rivalry between girls and boys. However, the material tackled in such lessons will inevitably be of a quite general nature, and there is arguably a need for more personal, specific gender issues to be addressed with pupils. For example, to encourage boys to develop their communication skills or to disrupt violent behaviour, or to encourage girls to be assertive. Writers such as Skeggs (1994) and Salisbury and Jackson (1996) have maintained the necessity of conducting such developmental work in single-sex groups. Pattman et al. (1998a) have shown how mixed group discussions can produce very different gender constructions from single-sex groups, and have suggested that it is easier for boys (and girls) to talk openly in single-sex groups. This raises the issue of the gender of the teacher; for example, can a female teacher tackle issues such as machismo and bullying with boys, or can a male teacher tackle problems of sexual harassment with girls? Pattman et al. (1998a) seem to suggest that many boys relish the opportunity of talking to a male authority figure and may communicate more openly with a man than they would do with a woman. However, the successful work with boys' groups carried out by Reay (1990a) suggests that a woman teacher can have equal success. Likewise, there is no reason why a male teacher cannot tackle issues such as assertiveness skills with girls (though it seems less appropriate and less effective for a male teacher to address issues of sexual harassment with girls' groups, where for instance girls might wish to share their experiences and be impeded by the presence of a male teacher).

It could be argued that the use of single-sex groups might illuminate gender polarity, and Reay (1998) found that parents were suspicious of single-sex groups. However, the advantages appear to outweigh the disadvantages, as some researchers have demonstrated single-sex groups to be an extremely effective way of addressing specific gender issues with pupils.[1]

The aim of such work is to encourage small groups of boys or girls to reflect on and engage with specific gender issues via exercises and/or discussion. In conducting such work, it is vital to create a 'safe' environment where pupils feel they can talk openly. Reay (1990a) and Salisbury and Jackson (1996) recommend negotiating and agreeing rules with the group concerned at the beginning of the group sessions. Salisbury and Jackson (1996) provide an outline of those rules that they have found to be the most useful. Their work was with boys, but their recommendations would be equally applicable to girls' groups.

1) No mocking or ridiculing of other members of the group
2) No interruptions or negative comments while someone else is speaking
3) Respect other people's contributions as you would like others to respect your stories

(Salisbury and Jackson, 1996, p. 233).

The scope of topics for such group work on gender is vast. However, from the findings presented in this book some of the most important areas might be the development of assertiveness and speculation skills for girls and the development of reflection, tenderness and communication among boys. The latter might include workshops on bullying, violence, sexism and homophobia too. Single-sex, small-group work is useful for getting pupils to think more closely about particular, sensitive topics and to discuss these issues in a relatively 'safe' environment. In leading these workshops it is important that teachers relate the discussion around these specific subjects back to the classroom work and discussion of the gender polarity, so that pupils can locate particular concerns (such as the expectation that boys do not articulate their personal feelings) within a broader understanding of oppositional gender constructions.

Teachers will find that some groups (and individuals within groups) need more encouragement than others to engage with the issue concerned. Salisbury and Jackson (1996) provide a refreshingly honest account of their work with groups of boys, documenting the frequent resistance they encountered from some boys. However, their candid account of the group work also reveals the enthusiasm and relief of many boys in being able to discuss the issues that Salisbury and Jackson were raising and to explore and develop their feelings and perspectives on these topics. Indeed, there are some very moving accounts of boys articulating their feelings and providing support for one another in these groups. Skeggs (1994) also provides a very positive account of the development and mutual empowerment that girls experienced in terms of understanding their sexuality and their experiences of sexual harassment.

There are many different approaches that can be taken to stimulate reflection and discussion in these groups, and the relative success of various methods may depend to an extent on the characters of the pupils involved. In some cases teachers may find it sufficient simply to introduce statements in order to spark off a discussion (for example in discussing gender stereotyping, flagging up statements such as 'boys don't cry'; for discussion, see Reay, 1990a). In other groups a structured session using role plays, discussion of prepared texts or specific exercises may be more appropriate. As I have observed, published work in this area is scant, and there has been little evaluation of the level of effectiveness of various techniques in working with young people around gender issues. Detailed suggestions for group work exercises are beyond the scope of this book and have not been tested by the author. However, Salisbury and Jackson (1996) provide an extensive catalogue of detailed suggestions and useful materials for using in workshops with boys on gender issues and aspects of their masculinity. The areas they cover are extremely diverse, ranging from homophobia and sexual harassment to the development of co-operative approaches and communication skills. Many of their suggestions and materials could be used directly, or adapted, for work with girls (and this is also true of some of the suggestions for group-work exercises in Davidson, 1990). Three of Salisbury and Jackson's different group work exercises are reproduced here in order to illustrate the diversity of possible approaches and to demonstrate the potential for stimulating and practicable work in this area.

1 Boys' Sexual Myths

Background: Boys relate to each other in an atmosphere in which a number of sexual myths serve to inhibit their capacity for shared feelings, intimacy and personal well-being. It is difficult for boys to admit their areas of sexual ignorance in front of their friends because the atmosphere engendered within the boys' club is one of being well versed in sexual matters. To admit ignorance or to be found out not knowing is to be the butt of put-downs and ridicule about a boy's sexuality and likely quality of performance. The atmosphere of jokey camaraderie to which the boys aspire is fuelled by the myths relating to sexual power and performance. All are assumed to be 'in the know' and, in so assuming, perpetuate the immutability of the myths still further.

The intention here is to state the myths under which boys operate and to find strategies that challenge them. It is important that this deconstruction takes place in a group atmosphere which allows for an acceptance of new learning and gives opportunities for new ways of behaving as a boy. So much of the way boys talk is about scoring, conquest and performance. Sex is used to shore up and confirm a shaky sense of masculine identity. This kind of knowledge is inextricably linked to being a real boy.

Aim: To enable boys to reconsider this bedrock of perceived masculinity so that sex can be seen as arising out of relationships, their closeness and contact.

Materials: 'The Myths' sheets, prepared using the statements below

Time: 30–45 minutes depending on size of group

What to do: Taking each myth in turn, ask the boys to put themselves on a continuum showing how much of their behaviour is informed by some belief in the truth of each statement.

Each boy speaks from the position he has found himself and shares his reasons for being there.

A lively discussion is likely as boys agree or disagree with each other. As facilitator, by using an interview technique with each boy, it will be possible to find out where the origins of these myths lie in each boy's life.

THE STATEMENTS

THE MYTHS

1 Penis size – the bigger the penis, the better the lover, the better the man.

employment. MacDonald (1999) also argues for meaningful work experience placement programmes in schools, geared to informing pupils about changing roles in adult and working life. However, Pickering observes that such strategies require a 'whole school approach': as well as informing pupils, boys (and girls) must be encouraged to develop the skills they need to move into new, non-traditional areas. In this respect, getting pupils to reflect on gender issues and to deconstruct oppositional constructions of gender, via the strategies suggested above, also have a crucial contribution to make.

Conclusion

This chapter has outlined some of the approaches that might be most effective for challenging and deconstructing pupils' oppositional gender constructions. The initial implementation of these strategies is unlikely to lead to immediate, dramatic change in pupils' constructions; therefore, teachers will need to pursue these approaches over a sustained period of time. However, the benefits of helping pupils to reflect upon and to challenge gender constructions should make these efforts worthwhile. It may serve to stem the excesses of gendered behaviour in the classroom and to empower pupils by providing the theoretical resources with which to challenge such constructions. It will enable pupils to reflect on their own gender constructions and the motivation behind them as well as providing information and understanding of the impact that these constructions have on their lives. This extra knowledge on the part of pupils should spur educational achievement, particularly if teaching strategies around gender issues are coupled with other forms of good teaching practice and a positive school ethos.

Appendix 1: Interview Schedule

1 What are your favourite subjects at school?
  Are these the ones you're good at?
2 What are your least favourite subjects at school?
  Are these the ones you're worst at?
3 Do you think that male and female students have the same ability at different subjects?
  If 'no', which subjects are involved and why?
4 What job do you hope to do in the future?
5 Are you planning to go on to further education?
6 Do you think that further education is important?
7 Can you say something about your learning style?
8 How about the learning approach of the class I've been watching?
9 What, in your view, is the ideal student like?
10 How far do you think you fit into this model?
11 Do you think being male or female makes a difference to this?
12 Do you think that being male or female makes a difference to your life generally in any way?
13 The ex-Education Minister Stephen Byers said that boys' 'laddish' behaviour is stopping boys from doing well at school – what do you think about that?

Appendix 2: Transcript Conventions

(.)	Short pause
(2)	Pause of two seconds duration (the digit changes to indicate length of pause in seconds)
=	To indicate lack of pause between speakers; for instance when one speaker gives way to another
[	
[	To indicate two people speaking at the same time
Italics	To indicate emphasized words
[…]	Inaudible speech
{}	Descriptive addition, e.g. {giggling}
:	To indicate a long-drawn-out word, e.g. No:o

Appendix 3: Attributes of an Ideal Pupil

Attributes	Number of times mentioned	
	Girls	Boys
Well behaved	2	5
Communicates with teacher/pupils	2	2
Not a goody-goody/swot	2	3
Neither best nor worst learner	1	1
Like her/him	0	3
Listens in class	7	6
A good learner	4	2
Punctual	2	6
Brainy/intelligent	3	3
Good looks/dress	1	3
Charisma/'personality'	1	3
Hard working	26	19
Role model to others	1	0
Able or interested in all subjects	3	2
Serious about work	3	3
Enjoys work	3	2
Has support from family and friends	1	0
Doesn't distract others or 'mess about'	5	4
Is boring/a swot	1	2
Attends school and lessons	4	3
Gets on with everyone	0	1
Doesn't get into trouble	2	5
High achiever	2	3
Good social life	6	4
Follows the teachers' instructions	0	1
Gets on with/respects the teacher	1	5
Not too quiet	1	1
Tries hard	7	3
There's no such thing	1	0
Asks for help when necessary	3	2
Polite	2	2
Does their homework	2	4
Self-motivated/disciplined	1	4
Doesn't care what others think	0	1
Ambitious	0	2
Fun/lively	4	1
Helps other pupils	1	0

Notes

1 Gender and Achievement: A Summary of Debates

1 For further reading, see the works of Sharpe (1976), Spender and Sarah (1980), Spender (1982) and Stanworth (1981).
2 Lee (1980) and Spender (1982) noted boys' lack of success at languages and queried the focus on girls' underachievement at maths and science in relation to the lack of focus on boys' underachievement in other areas of the curriculum.
3 The 1998 National League Tables show that a number of exclusive girls' private schools have now outstripped those of boys in terms of GCSE achievement and now stand at the top of the league tables.

2 Theoretical Perspectives of Gender Identity

1 For a fuller discussion of the limitations of socialization and sex role theories, see Davies (1989), Connell (1987; 1995) or Francis (1998a).
2 For elaboration see, for example, Francis (1997a; 1998a,c).
3 In the paper 'Modernist reductionism or post-modernist relativism: shall we move on?' (1999b), I set out the reasons why feminism cannot be seen to be other than a modernist theory, building on the theoretical work of Balbus (1987) and Assiter (1996).

3 Gendered Classroom Culture

1 See Belotti (1975), Clarricoates (1980), Stanworth (1981) and Spender (1982) for a discussion of teachers' gender constructions and consequent negative perceptions of their female pupils. See Younger and Warrington (1996) and Pickering (1997) for a discussion of teachers' construction of male pupils as disruptive.
2 For any international readers that have not come across this term, a full account can be found in Chapter 7.
3 Lees (1993), Herbert (1989), Jones and Mahony (1989) and Holly (1989) have catalogued the sexist abuse and sexual harassment that girls and female teachers experience in the secondary school. Lees, particularly, discusses the ways in which these practices are used by males to regulate and police female behaviour.
4 These examples all contain the words 'shut up'. A note must be made on the (frequent) use of this phrase among young and 'streetwise' people in South

London, in that their way of saying it expresses far more feeling that the actual text suggests. The pupils have a way of saying 'shut up' that suggests utter disdain and sneering disgust for the person being told to shut up.

4 Young People's Constructions of Gender and Status

1 See Francis (1997b; 1998c) for elaboration.
2 Jamaican patois for sanitary towel/tampon.

5 Young People's Talk about Gender and Studentship

1 The concept of 'Girl Power' was promoted by female pop group the Spice Girls. This glossy version of feminism presented young women as assertive and ambitious while retaining 'feminine' glamour.

6 Young People's Views of the Importance of Gender and Education for their Lives

1 Research by Francis (1996), Lightbody and Durndell (1996), Whitehead (1996) and Pickering (1997) shows that boys' career and subject choices are more gender stereotypical than are those of girls.

7 Young People's Talk about Gender and Behaviour

1 The final question ran: "The ex-Education Minister Stephen Byers said that boys' 'laddish behaviour' is stopping them from doing well at school – what do you think about that?"
2 'Bad' here meaning tough; see also Hewitt (1988).

8 Discussion: Gender, Achievement and Status

1 See also the findings of researchers such as Mac an Ghaill (1994) and Sewell (1997) for a discussion of academically oriented groups of boys.
2 See, for example, the findings on gender and work roles by Nemerowicz (1979), Furnham and Stacey (1991) and Francis (1996, 1998a), and on gender roles in the family by Furnham and Stacey (1991), Lees (1993) and Edley and Wetherell (1999).
3 For an explanation of this position, see particularly Foucault (1980).

9 Teaching Strategies for the Future

1 For examples of work on gender issues in single-sex groups, see Reay (1990a,b), Skeggs (1994) and Salsibury and Jackson (1996).

References

Adler, A. and Adler, P. (1998) *Peer Power: Preadolescent Culture and Identity*, New Brunswick: Rutgers University Press.

Ainley, P. (1993) *Class and Skill*, London: Cassell.

Anyon, J. (1983) 'Intersections of Gender and Class', in S. Walker and L. Barton (eds) *Gender, Class and Education*, London: Falmer.

Arnot, M., David, M. and Weiner, G. (1999) *Closing the Gender Gap*, Cambridge: Polity Press.

Assiter, A. (1996) *Enlightened Women: Modernist Feminism in a Postmodern Age*, London: Routledge.

Balbus, I. (1987) 'Disciplining women: Michel Foucault and the power of feminist discourse', in S. Benhabib and D. Cornell (eds) *Feminism as Critique*, Cambridge: Polity Press.

Barker, B. (1997) 'Girls' world or anxious times: what's really happening at school in the gender war?' *Educational Review*, 49: 221–7.

Belotti, E. (1975) *Little Girls*, London: Writers and Readers Publishing Co-op.

Benskin, A. (1994) *Black Children and Underachievement in Urban Schools*, London: Minerva.

Billig, M., Condor, S., Edwards, D., Gane, M., Middleton, D., and Radley, A. (1988) *Ideological Dilemmas*, London: Sage.

Bleach, K. (1998a) 'Why the likely lads lag behind', in K. Bleach (ed.) *Raising Boys' Achievement in Schools*, Stoke-on-Trent: Trentham Books.

Bleach, K. (1998b) 'What difference does it make?' in K. Bleach (ed.) *Raising Boys' Achievement in Schools*, Stoke-on-Trent: Trentham Books.

Blyth, A. (1992) 'Themes and dimensions: icing or spicing?', in G. Hall (ed.) *Themes And Dimensions of the National Curriculum*, London: Kogan Page.

Bourdieu, P. and Passeron, J. (1979) *Reproduction in Education, Society and Culture*, London: Sage.

Brighouse, T. (1998) 'Foreword', in K. Bleach (ed.) *Raising Boys' Achievement in Schools*, Stoke-on-Trent: Trentham Books.

Buckingham, D. (1993) *Children Talking Television*, Lewes: Falmer.

Burr, V. (1995) *An Introduction to Social Constructionism*, London: Routledge.

Butler, J. (1990) *Gender Trouble*, New York: Routledge.

Carspecken, P. (1996) *Critical Ethnography in Educational Research*, London: Routledge.

Cealey Harrison, W. and Hood-Williams, J. (1998) 'More varieties than Heinz: social categories and sociality in Humphries, Hammersley and Beyond', *Social Research Online*, 3, 1.

Clark, D. (1998) 'Gender gap', *Management in Education*, 12: 9–14.

Clarricoates, C. (1980) 'The importance of being Ernest... Emma... Tom... Jane', in R. Deem (ed.) *Schooling for Women's Work*, London: Routledge and Kegan Paul.

Cohen, M. (1998) 'A habit of healthy idleness: boy's underachievement in historical perspective', in D. Epstein, J. Elwood, V. Hey and J. Maw (eds) *Failing Boys?* Buckingham: Open University Press.

Cohen, S. (1973) *Folk Devils and Moral Panics: the Creation of Mods and Rockers*, London: Paladin.

Connell, R. (1987) *Gender and Power*, Cambridge: Polity Press.

Connell, R. (1995) *Masculinities*, Cambridge: Polity Press.

Connolly, P. (1998) *Racism, Gender Identities and Young Children*, London: Routledge.

Crompton, R. (1997) *Women and Work in Modern Britain*, Oxford: Oxford University Press.

Davies, B. (1989) *Frogs and Snails and Feminist Tales*, Sydney: Allen and Unwin.

Davies, B. (1993) *Shards of Glass*, Sydney: Allen and Unwin.

Denscombe, I. (1995) 'Explorations in group interviews: an evaluation of a reflexive and partisan approach', *British Educational Research Journal*, 21, 2: 131–8.

Department for Education and Employment (1998a) *Moving On: Pathways Taken By Young People Beyond 16: The Careers Service Activity Survey*, London: Department for Education and Employment.

Department for Education and Employment (1998b) 'Playing for Success' (outline paper), London, Department of Education and Employment.

Dixon, C. (1996) "Having a laugh, having a fight': masculinity and the conflicting needs of the self in Design and Technology', *International Studies of Sociology of Education*, 6, 2: 147–66.

Edley, N. and Wetherell, M. (1999) 'Imagined futures: young men's talk about fatherhood and domestic life', *British Journal of Social Psychology*, 38: 181–94.

Edwards, A. and Westgate, P. (1994) *Investigating Classroom Talk* (Second Edition), London: Falmer.

Epstein, D. (1993) *Changing Classroom Cultures*, Stoke-on-Trent: Trentham Books.

— (1998) 'Real boys don't work: 'underachievement', masculinity and the harassment of 'sissies'', in D. Epstein, J. Elwood, V. Hey and J. Maw (eds) *Failing Boys?* Buckingham: Open University Press.

Epstein, D., Elwood, J., Hey, V. and Maw, J. (1998) 'Schoolboy frictions: feminism and 'failing' boys', in D. Epstein, J. Elwood, V. Hey and J. Maw (eds) *Failing Boys?* Buckingham: Open University Press.

Fernie, S. and Metcalfe, D. (1996) *Low Pay and Minimum Wages: The British Evidence*, London: Centre for Economic Performance.

Foucault, M. (1980) *Power/Knowledge: Selected Interviews and Other Writings, 1972–1977*, New York: Pantheon.

— (1992) *Politics, Philosophy, Culture: interviews and other writings, 1977–1984*, London: Routledge.

Francis, B. (1996) 'Doctor/nurse, teacher/caretaker: children's gendered choice of adult occupation in interviews and role play' (1996) *British Journal of Education and Work*, 9, 3: 47–58.

— (1997a) 'Power play: children's constructions of gender and power' *Gender and Education*, 9, 2: 179–91.

— (1997b) Discussing discrimination: children's constructions of sexism between pupils in primary school' *British Journal of Sociology of Education*, 18, 4: 519–33.

— (1998a) *Power Plays: primary school children's constructions of gender, power and adult work,* Stoke-on-Trent: Trentham Books.

— (1998b) 'Degrees of gender: gendered patterns in undergraduate academic success and failure, and the methodological difficulties in researching this area', presented at 'Gendering the Millennium' International Conference, University of Dundee, 1998.

— (1998c) 'Oppositional positions: children's constructions of gender in talk and role plays based on adult occupation', *Educational Research*, 40, 1: 31–43.

— (1999a) 'Lads, Lasses and (New) Labour: 14–16 year old students' responses to the 'laddish behaviour and boys' underachievement' debate', *British Journal of Sociology of Education*, 20, 3: 357–373.

— (1999b) 'Modernist reductionism or post-modernist relativism: can we move on? An evaluation of the arguments in relation to feminist educational research', *Gender & Education*, 11, 4: 381–393.

— (1999c) An investigation of the discourses children draw on in their constructions of gender, *Journal of Applied Social Psychology*, 29, 2: 300–316.

— (2000) 'The Gendered Subject: students' subject preferences and discussions of gender and subject ability', *Oxford Review of Education*. 26, 1: 35–48.

Frater, G. (1998) 'Boys and literacy', in K. Bleach (ed.) *Raising Boys' Achievement in Schools*, Stoke-on-Trent: Trentham Books.

Furnham, D. and Stacey, R (1991) *Young People's Understanding of Society*, London: Routledge.

Gaskell, J. (1992) *Gender Matters From School to Work*, Buckingham: Open University Press.

Giddens, A. (1992) *The Transformation of Intimacy*, Cambridge: Polity Press.

Gorard, S, Rees, G., and Salisbury, J. (1999) 'Reappraising the apparent underachievement of boys at school', *Gender and Education*, 11, 4: 441–54.

Griffin, C. (1998) 'Representations of youth and the 'boys' underachievement' debate: just the same old stories?', presented at 'Gendering the Millennium' International Conference, University of Dundee, 1998.

The Guardian (1998a) 'Editorial: grim reading for males' (6/1/98) pp. 12–13.

Halford, S., Savage, M. and Witz, A. (1997) *Gender, Careers and Organisations*, Basingstoke: Macmillan.

Herbert, C. (1989) *Talking of Silence – The Sexual Harassment of Schoolgirls*, London: Falmer.

Hewitt, R. (1988) *White Talk, Black Talk*, Cambridge: Cambridge University Press.

Higher Education Statistical Agency (1999) *Research Data Pack 3*, Cheltenham: Higher Education Statistical Agency.

Hill Collins, P. (1991) *Black Feminist Thought*, London: Routledge.

Holland, J., Ramazanoglu, C., Sharpe, S. and Thomson, R. (1998) *The Male in the Head*, London, Tufnell Press.

Holly, L. (ed.) (1989) *Girls and Sexuality*, Buckingham: Open University Press.

Howe, C. (1997) *Gender and Classroom Interaction: A Research Review*, Edinburgh: SCRE.

Jones, C. and Mahony, P. (eds) (1989) *Learning Our Lines*, London: The Women's Press.

Jordan, E. (1995) 'Fighting boys and fantasy play: the construction of masculinity in the early years of school', *Gender and Education*, 7, 1: 69–86.

Kenway, J. et al. (1994) Making 'hope practical' rather than 'despair convincing': feminist poststructuralism, gender reform and social change', *British Journal of Sociology of Education*, 15, 2: 187–210.

Kerfoot, D. and Whitehead, S. (1998) 'W(h)ither hegemonic masculinity?' presented at 'Gendering the Millennium' International Conference, University of Dundee, 1998.

Lee, A. (1980) 'Together we learn to read and write: sexism and literacy', in D. Spender and E. Sarah (eds) *Learning to Lose*, London: The Women's Press.

Lees, S. (1993) *Sugar and Spice*, London: Penguin.

Lightbody, P. and Durndell, A. (1996) 'Gendered career choice: is sex-stereotyping the cause or the consequence?' *Educational Studies*, 22, 2: 133–46.

Maccoby, A. and Jacklin, C. (1974) *The Psychology of Sex Differences*, Stanford, CA: Stanford University Press.

Mac an Ghaill, M. (1994) *The Making of Men*, Buckingham: Open University Press.

— (1999) ' "New" cultures of training: emerging male (hetero)sexual identities', *British Educational Research Journal*, 25, 4: 427–44.

MacDonald, A., Saunders, L. and Benefield, P. (1999) *Boys' Achievement, Progress, Motivation and Participation: Issues Raised by the Literature*, Berkshire: NFER.

MacInnes, J. (1998) *The End of Masculinity*, Buckingham: Open University Press.

Mahony, P. (1998) 'Girls will be girls and boys will be first', in D. Epstein, J. Elwood, V. Hey and J. Maw (eds.) *Failing Boys?*, Buckingham: Open University Press.

Martino, W. (1999) '"Cool boys", "party animals", "squids" and "poofters": interrogating the dynamics and politics of adolescent masculinities in school', *British Journal of Sociology of Education*, 20, 2: 240–63.

Mirza, H. (1992) *Young, Female and Black*, London: Routledge.

Morris, K. (1997) '*Girl power: the lives and friendships of a group of adolescent girls in a rural area*', unpublished PhD Thesis, University of Bristol.

Nemerowicz, G. (1979) *Children's Perceptions of Gender and Work Roles*, New York: Praegar Publishers.

The Observer Magazine (1999) 'The Problem With Boys', (20/6/99) 14–24.

Paechter, C. (1998) *Educating the Other*, London: Falmer.

Panorama (1994) 'The Future is Female' (24/2/94).

Pattman, R., Phoenix, A. and Frosh, S. (1998a) Lads, Machos and Others: developing 'boy centred' research, *Journal of Youth Studies*, 1: 125–42.

—— (1998b) '"Boys have a heart but they don't think that much"– maturity, immaturity and how boys and girls position themselves and each other in interviews', presented at 'Gendering the Millennium' international Conference, University of Dundee, 1998.

Pattman, R., Phoenix, A., Frosh, S. And Patel, R. (1999) ' "What's the point of eleven men running up and down a bit of grass kicking a ball"?: Football talk and the identities of boys and girls', presented at the ESA Conference, Free University, Amsterdam, August 1999.

Penny, V. (1998) 'Raising boys' achievement in English', in K. Bleach (ed.) *Raising Boys' Achievement in Schools*, Stoke-on-Trent: Trentham Books.

Pickering, J. (1997) *Raising Boys' Achievement*, Stafford: Network Educational Press.

Phoenix, A. (1987) 'Theories of gender and black families', in G. Weiner and M. Arnot (eds.) *Gender Under Scrutiny*, Milton Keynes: Open University Press.

Phoenix, A., Frosh, S. and Pattman, R. (forthcoming) '"You're not popular if you work hard": the intersection of hegemonic masculinities and education for 11– 14 year old boys in London schools'.

Power, S., Edwards, A., Whitty, G. and Wigfall, V. (1998) 'Schoolboys and schoolwork: gender identification and academic achievement', *Journal of Inclusive Education*, 2, 2: 135–153.

Qualifications and Curriculum Authority (1998) *Can do Better...Raising Boys' Achievements in English,* London: Qualification and Curriculum Authority.

Rampton, B. (1995) *Crossing: Language and Ethnicity Among Adolescents*, London: Longman.

Raphael Reed, L. (1998) 'Zero tolerance: gender performance and school failure', in D. Epstein, J. Elwood, V. Hey and J. Maw (eds.) *Failing Boys?,* Buckingham: Open University Press.

Reay, D. (1990a) 'Girl's groups as a component of anti-sexist practice: one primary school's experience, *Gender and Education*, 2, 1: 37–47.

—— (1990b) 'Working with boys', *Gender and Education,* 2, 3: 269–281.

—— (1998) *Class Work*, London: UCL Press.

—— (1999) 'Sugar and spice and all things nice? Gender discourses and girls' cultures in the primary classroom', presented at 'Voices in Gender and Education' Conference, University of Warwick, 1999.

Redman, P. (1998) 'Romantic heroes: schooling, the unconscious and the narrative production of heterosexual masculinities', presented at 'Gendering the Millennium' International Conference, University of Dundee, 1998.

Rees, T. (1999) *Mainstreaming Equality in the European Union*, New York: Routledge.

Regan, C. (1998) 'Boys' underachievement? Not the real question', *Socialist Teacher*, 6: 20–1.

Riddell, S. (1989) 'Pupils, resistance and gender codes', *Gender and Education*, 1, 2: 183–96.

—— (1992) *Polities and the Gender of the Curriculum*, London: Routledge.

Robson, C. (1993) *Real World Research*, London: Blackwell.

Salisbury, J. and Jackson, D. (1996) *Challenging Macho Values*, London: Falmer Press.

Sampson, E. (1989) 'The deconstruction of the self', in J. Shotter and Gergen (eds) *Texts of Identity*, London: Sage.

Sewell, T. (1997) *Black Masculinities and Schooling: How black boys survive modern schooling*, Stoke-on-Trent: Trentham Books.

— (1998) 'Loose canons: exploding the myth of the 'black macho' lad', in D. Epstein, J. Elwood, V. Hey and J. Maw (eds) *Failing Boys?* Buckingham: Open University Press.

Sharpe, S. (1974) (Second edition 1994) *Just Like a Girl*, Harmondsworth: Penguin.

Shkedi, A. (1998) 'Teachers' attitudes towards research: a challenge for qualitative researchers', *Qualitative Studies in Education*, 11, 4: 559–77.

Skeggs, B. (1994) 'Situating the production of feminist methodology', in M. Maynard and J. Purvis (eds) *Researching Women's Lives From a Feminist Perspective*, London: Taylor and Francis.

Skelton, C. (1997) 'Primary boys and hegemonic masculinities', *British Journal of Sociology of Education*, 18: 349–68.

— (1998) 'Feminism and research into masculinities and schooling', *Gender and Education*, 10: 217–27.

— (1999) 'Becoming macho: infant boys, masculinities and schooling', presented at 'Voices in Gender and Education' conference, University of Warwick, 1999.

— (2000) 'Constructing dominant masculinity and negotiating the "male gaze"', *International Journal of Inclusive Education* (in press).

Smaling, A. (1993) 'Open-mindedness and open-heartedness and dialogical openness: the dialectics of openings and closures', presented at 'Openness in Research' congress, University of Utrecht.

Smith, J. (1998) *Different for Girls*, London: Chatto & Windus.

Soper, K. (1990) *Troubled Pleasures*, London: Verso.

Spender, D. (1982) *Invisible Women: The Schooling Scandal*, London: Writers and Readers.

Spender, D. and Sarah, E. (eds.) (1980) *Learning to Lose: Sexism and Education*, London: The Women's Press.

Stanley, L. and Wise, S. (1993) *Breaking Out Again: Feminist Ontology and Epistemology*, London: Routledge.

Stanworth, M. (1981) *Gender and Schooling*, London: Hutchinson.

Swan, B. (1998) 'Teaching boys and girls in separate classes at Shenfield High School, Brentford, in K. Bleach (ed.) *Raising Boys' Achievement in Schools*, Stoke-on-Trent: Trentham Books.

Times Educational Supplement, (1998) 'Failing Boys "Public Burden Number One" ', (27/11/98) p. 1.

Thomas, K. (1990) *Gender and Subject in Higher Education*, Buckingham: Open University Press.

Thorne, B. (1993) *Gender Play: Girls and Boys in School*, Buckingham: Open University Press.

164 *References*

Tomlinson, S. (1997) 'Education 14–19: Divided and Divisive', in S. Tomlinson (ed.) *Education 14–19: Critical Perspectives,* London: The Athlone Press.

Volman, M. and Ten Dam, G. (1998) 'Equal but different: contradictions in the development of gender identity', *British Journal of Sociology of Education*, 19: 529–45.

Wallace, M. (1979) *Black Macho and the Myth of the Superwoman*, London: J.Calder.

Walkerdine, V. (1988) *The Mastery of Reason*, London: Routledge.

— (1990) *Schoolgirl Fictions*, London: Verso.

— (1997) *Daddy's Girl*, Basingstoke: Macmillan Press.

Walkerdine, V. and the Girls and Mathematics Unit (1989) *Counting Girls Out*, London: Virago.

Walkerdine, V. and Lucey, H. (1989) *Democracy in the Kitchen*, London: Virago.

Weeks, J. (1995) *Invented Moralities*, Cambridge: Polity Press.

Whitehead, J. (1996) 'Sex stereotypes, gender identity and subject choice at 'A'-level', *Educational Research*, 38, 2: 147–60.

— (1998) 'Masculinity, motivation and academic success: a paradox', presented at 'Gendering the Millennium' International Conference, University of Dundee, 1998

Whitehead, S. (1999) 'A desire to be: the pursuit of ideal representations by the masculine subject', presented at 'Voices in Gender and Education, University of Warwick, 1999.

Whyte, J. (1986) *Beyond the Wendy House: sex-role stereotyping in primary schools*, York: Longman.

Willis, P. (1977) *Learning to Labour: How working class kids get working class jobs,* Aldershot: Saxon House.

Wing, A. (1997) 'How can children be taught to read differently? *Bill's New Frock* and the hidden curriculum', *Gender and Education*, 9, 4: 491–504.

Wragg, E. (1994) *An Introduction to Classroom Observation*, London: Routledge.

Yates, L. (1997) 'Gender equity and the boys debate: what sort of challenge is it?', *British Journal of Sociology of Education*, 18: 337–47.

Yeoman, E. (1999) '"How does it get into my imagination?": elementary school children's inter-textual knowledge and gendered storylines', *Gender and Education*, 11, 4: 427–40.

Young, M. and Spours, K. (1998) 14–19 Education: legacy, opportunities and challenges, *Oxford Review of Education*, 24: 83–97.

Younger, M. and Warrington, M. (1996) 'Differential achievement of girls and boys at GCSE: some observations from the perspective of one school', *British Journal of Sociology of Education*, 17: 299–314.

Younger, M., Warrington, M and Williams, J. (1999) 'The gender gap and classroom interactions: reality and rhetoric?', *British Journal of Sociology of Education*, 20, 3: 325–42.

Index

ability: gender and 10, 68–9, 74, 120–1
appearance: concern with 45–6, 48, 101, 103
aggression: verbal (*see also* verbal abuse) 41–2, 48; physical 42–4, 48

bullying 40, 44, 133

career 80, 88–90, 92–3, 108–9, 121, 124, 151
'class clowns' 55, 57
classroom observation 21, 23, 25–28, 30, 33–4, 37, 94
computers 45

deconstruction 20, 140-2
desire 38, 106
discipline 33, 64, 68, 77–8, 115, 120, 137–8
discourse: analysis 19–20, 96, 114; categories of 9-11, 14, 69–70, 73–5, 79, 82, 91, 95, 105, 108, 114, 123, 141
dominance 23; female 119; male: of classroom space 11, 31, 118, 120, 123; of curriculum 11, 123; of teacher time 11, 77, 118, 120, 123; other 49–50, 94

equal opportunities 68, 70, 124, 141; discourse 69, 81, 112, 114–15, 141; programmes 88, 130
ethnicity 11–12, 16, 22–4, 80, 96

female fear 82

femininities 14–16
femininity 5, 7, 14-17; construction of 13, 44, 46, 48, 50, 55, 58, 65, 71, 78, 93, 117, 121, 128, 139; cultural ideal 44, 48, 121
feminist: research 4–6, 11, 13–14, 19, 25, 27, 123; theory 14, 19-20
football 44–5, 83, 85, 90, 102–3, 133
friendship 73–4, 99–100, 131
further education 90–1, 93, 121

GCSE: explanation of 1; achievement at 1–2, 6–12, 21–3, 69, 88, 93, 120–2, 124, 156
gender: cultures 30, 32, 48–9, 73, 94, 130; dichotomy 15–17, 19–20, 90, 116, 134, 141; difference 4, 18–19, 22–3, 30–1, 35, 48, 69–71, 80, 91, 98, 105, 113; differences in exam performance 6–12 (*see also* GCSE); discourse 9–11 (*see also* discourse); discrimination 4–6, 76–7, 81–8, 92–3, 110, 121, 124, 137–8; essentialism (inherent difference) 71; 105; identity (theory of) 1, 13–18; role maintenance 122, 141; stereotypes 32, 46, 48, 81, 88, 134
gender construction 14–20, 22; contradiction 52–4, 75, 113; responses according to 46–8; 'sensible selfless' 50–8, 61, 65, 118–19; 'silly selfish' 50–61, 65, 118–19

heterosexuality 29, 33; attraction 105–6, 115–16; construction of 35–9, 49

higher education 92–3, 121
homophobia 39–41, 118
humour 57, 65, 118

ideal pupil 66–8
immaturity 39, 50–1, 70
interviews 21, 28–9

job choice 88–90

lad: definition 94–5; 'laddish'
  behaviour 38, 57, 65, 95–116, 118,
  120, 122–25, 129–30, 138, 143,
  157

masculinity 14–17; black; 38;
  construction of 14–18, 38, 40–2,
  44, 47–8, 50, 54–5, 57–8, 65, 71–2,
  93, 94–117, 120, 122–31, 133–5,
  138–40, 143; crisis of 1–2, 7–8,
  113, 125–7; cultural ideal of 128–
  30; hegemonic 14, 16; subjugated
  16
masculinities 14–16
maturity 50–1, 61–2, 71, 100, 104,
  112, 118
misogyny 18, 29, 40–1, 103, 118, 131
modernism 156

National Curriculum 6–8, 23, 142

observation (*see* classroom
  observation)
oppositional constructions 50, 58, 65,
  102–3, 116, 128
post-structuralism 14; theory 19–20;
  teaching about 140
power 128; use of 3–4, 61, 118;

differences 9, 18–20, 25, 35, 40,
  50, 61, 81

racism 133
researcher: impact on research 25–6,
  28; impact of research on 27–8
reading 134, 137, 142
resistance 62–5, 72, 101, 125

school: culture 40, 72; description of
  21–2
sexual harassment 29
sexuality: construction of 35–9
social class 11–12, 22, 122
social constructionism 19
status 55, 58, 72, 117–18

teacher: compliance in gender
  constructions 57; constructions of
  gender 31–5, 75, 133, 156
teaching strategies 132; for improved
  achievement 133–52; to check
  against discrimination in classroom
  practice 48–9, 138–9; to
  deconstruct the gender dichotomy
  49, 142–51
television 74

underachievement 2, 5–8, 10, 14, 65,
  70, 74, 79, 95, 102, 122–3, 132–6,
  138, 143, 156

verbal abuse 40–3, 118; terms of 40–1
violence: female 43–4; male 42–3

work 14, 81, 84, 86–7, 108, 121;
  changes in the work market 6–7,
  87, 109, 125, 151; gender
  differences 7, 92, 125, 151